DEATH IN THE ARDENNES

Jean-Michel Steg

Translated by Joshua Sigal

UNIVERSITY OF
BUCKINGHAM
PRESS

Published by University of Buckingham Press,
an imprint of Legend Times Group
51 Gower Street
London WC1E 6HJ
info@unibuckinghampress.com
www.unibuckinghampress.com

First published in French in 2013 by Éditions Fayard

© Jean-Michel Steg, 2013, 2021
Translation © Joshua Sigal, 2013

The right of the above author and translator to be identified as the author and translator of this work has been asserted in accordance with the Copyright, Designs and Patents Act 1988. British Library Cataloguing in Publication Data available.

ISBN (paperback): 9781800310896
ISBN (ebook): 9781800310902

Cover design: Ditte Løkkegaard
Printed by Lightning Source

All rights reserved. No part of this publication may be reproduced, stored in or introduced into a retrieval system, or transmitted, in any form, or by any means electronic, mechanical, photocopying, recording or otherwise, without the prior permission of the publisher. Any person who commits any unauthorised act in relation to this publication may be liable to criminal prosecution and civil claims for damages.

To Diane, of course

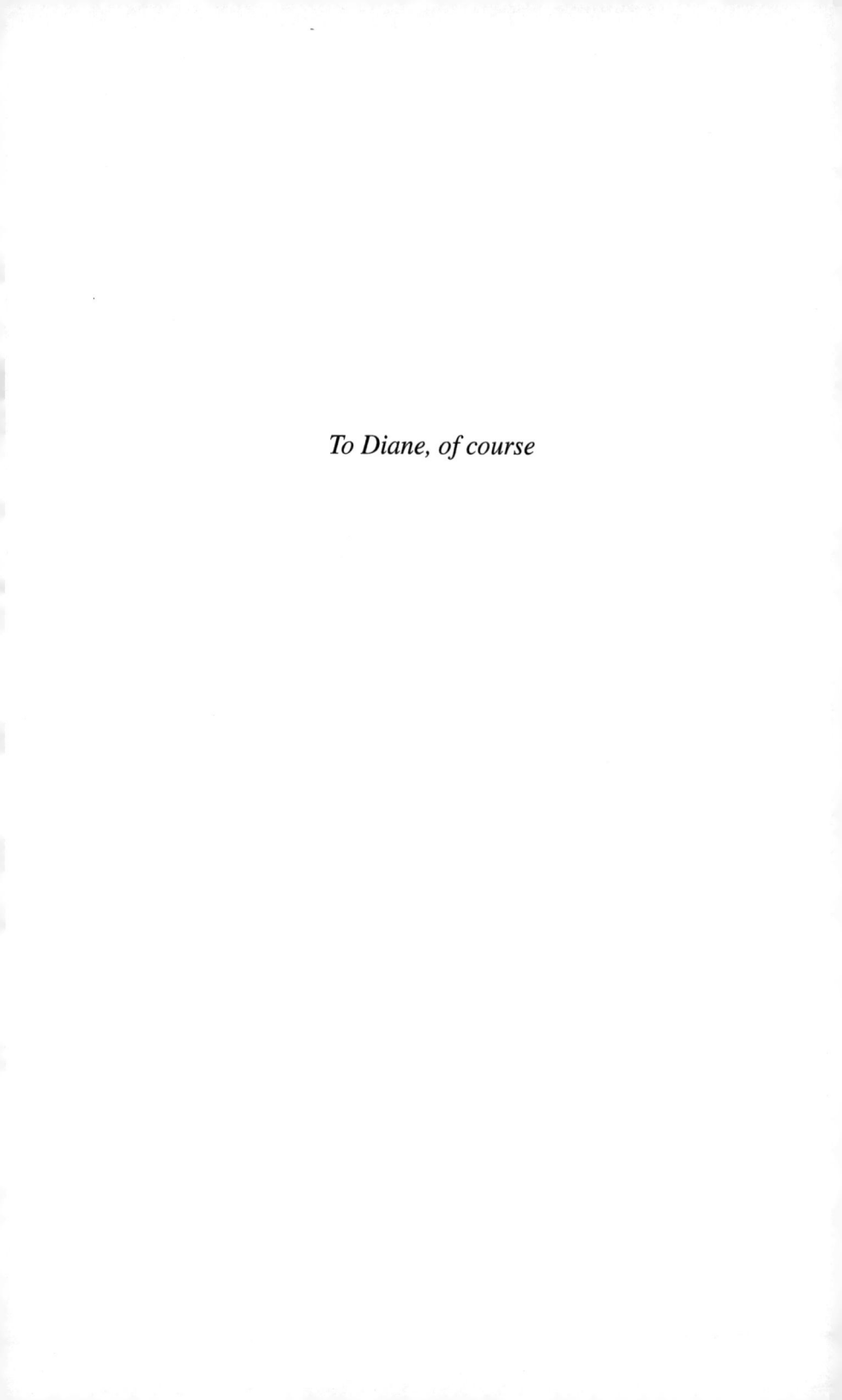

CONTENTS

Foreword......1
Preface......6
Chapter 1......12
An Unknown Catastrophe
Chapter 2......23
The Battle of Rossignol: An Hour-by-Hour Reconstruction
Chapter 3......47
From Frankfurt to Rossignol
Chapter 4......73
Weapons and Organization
Chapter 5......86
Entry into War
Chapter 6......111
The Battle of the Ardennes
Chapter 7......125
The Battle of Charleroi and the Retreat
Chapter 8......138
Civilians in German Cross Hairs
Chapter 9......158
Why So Many Dead?
Epilogue......174
Rossignol, 23 June 2012
Acknowledgements......180
Bibliography......182
Tables and Appendices......187
Endnotes......194

FOREWORD

As summed up pointedly by the writer of the following pages, this is a book about death, dealing with one of the tragic days of battle in the period 20–24 August 1914, during which about 40,000 Frenchmen lost their lives. More precisely, its focus is the bloodiest day of them all, 22 August 1914, on which 27,000 died. It was near Rossignol, in the Belgian Ardennes, that this horrible tragedy had its most severe impact. Jean-Michel Steg therefore takes this violent epicentre of the day's events as his main subject.

For at least ten years, the question of the unprecedented level of casualties during these August days has been a source of fascination for him, forgotten days themselves inseparable from something else that has also slipped from collective memory: the losses occasioned by the battles. A fine example of a 'problem of history' applied to the beginnings of the Great War and which led the author, who comes from a profession quite different from the humanities and social sciences, to the study of war history.

Jean-Michel Steg explains very well the varied reasons that such an extreme peak of violence has faded from memory. Briefly, we can say that the Battle of the Marne in early September 1914, itself extremely deadly, but from which the French and British emerged triumphant, blotted out the bloody defeats during the Battle of the Frontiers the previous month. In addition, too many direct witnesses were annihilated immediately or died soon afterwards to provide adequate accounts, while French military officials certainly had no interest in reviewing their actions during this episode. Furthermore, the subsequent digging of trenches over a 700-kilometre stretch of the front obliterated, if not the victory at the Marne, at least the initial phase of the conflict, known as the 'war of movement'. A new type of war – although it had first been used on a large scale during the Russo-Japanese War, and specifically at the Battle of Mukden in February-March 1905 – a type of combat rather close to an open siege war over a front of several hundred kilometres, with its very particular horrors, would thus supplant others, those of the summer of 1914. In the same time and space, one war replaced another, first in the facts and then in collective memory. Historians themselves have not been spared by this shift.

However, in recent years, interest has been rekindled in these first days, in the first weeks of this worldwide conflict, and it is very possible that the recent centenary of the war, with a large number of commemorative events having taken place in the summer of 2014, has helped direct attention to this precise moment of the massive conflict. The atrocities that accompanied the German invasion of Belgium, which the historians John Horne and Alan Kramer have brought so clearly into focus,[1] have thus been rediscovered and entirely revisited: their inclusion in Jean-Michel's Steg's book, through a precise analysis of the massacre of 383 Belgian civilians (men, women and children), which occurred in the Charleroi suburb of Tamines on 22 August 1914, is a direct result of Horne and Kramer's major contribution to the historiography of 1914–18. A new military history by Damien Baldin and

Emmanuel Saint-Fuscien has in turn taken up the events at and near Charleroi in this same week of August 1914.[2] This work by Jean-Michel Steg is fully in keeping with the overall trend in the rediscovery of this period of the war from an event-based perspective.

His aim here is twofold. Taking as his starting point the extreme confusion that reigned at the scene on 22 August 1914, Steg seeks to craft a narrative able to make sense of what was actually playing out for the soldiers on that day. At a time when all the armies of France were engaged over a front 400 kilometres long, when between 400,000 and 600,000 French troops were seeing combat, our author recounts the fate of two of the Fourth Army's colonial divisions in the Ardennes, outside the village of Rossignol. He poignantly describes the courage of the men under a deluge of bullets and artillery shells. Steg also aptly conveys the high command's mental confusion, brought completely to its wits' end by the experience of this new type of war, which nothing could have prepared it to confront. Lastly, he speaks of the extreme devastation wreaked upon junior officers, who had been persuaded, in the absence of instructions from on high, that their duty was to remain in full view in front of their men in order to set a courageous example and prevent panic.

At Rossignol on 22 August, a long-standing battle ethos, requiring that the enemy be faced in an upright posture (whose importance throughout history has been compellingly argued by Georges Vigarello[3]), seeking not invisibility but instead the greatest visibility possible, conveyed the resilience of an imagined model of war and the fecundity of an age-old set of notions about the self in war. The bodily *hexis* (fixed tendency) of so many French officers that day, depriving the rank and file of nearly all of their immediate superiors, who were either wounded or killed, keenly illustrates the shock at this time between two ages of war, between two ages of combat. On that fateful day of 22 August, and even though the German troops sustained such heavy losses that they also remained unconvinced of their victory, it was their French adversaries who, precisely as a result of this failed transition early in the war, actually paid the highest price. For this reason, Steg is right to suggest that 22 August marks France's true entry into the twentieth century – certainly one among other possible entries. But, in any case, this entry was by way of a 'first catastrophe',[4] through an originating disaster. After commemorating its centenary, the consciousness we all have, especially in France, that we trace our origins back to this watershed moment seems never to have been so acute.

One of the reasons for the high human toll of the events of 22 August, apart from the fact that the French military medical service was overwhelmed (the ratio of casualties was one dead for every two wounded) – also setting aside the Germans' dense firepower and their more effective implementation of combat resources (served, in addition, by a less rigid chain of command) – and perhaps one of the most difficult to admit now, is that at the time military losses did not have the importance we would be likely to give them today. The losses of 22 August are appalling precisely because the French army 'made no particular effort to minimize them', as Jean-Michel Steg states quite simply. It is historians who strive, after the fact, to count the dead, wounded and missing in action, and those taken prisoner. And it is also historians who raise their voices in response to the staggering figures they discover, such as those discussed in this book. But in 1914, what mattered more for French military leaders was the remaining fighting force, its physical and moral state, its supplies of ammunition, all likely to influence the effectiveness of combat on the following days. To which might be added their expectation that the war would be abbreviated in duration, which was correlated with their acceptance of very high losses, although concentrated over a short period.

On a still more general level, it is important to remember that French society had long been prepared to consider death in warfare as a normal element of individual and collective destiny. Certainly, combat deaths between 20 and 24 August went far beyond even the most sombre predictions. But these figures did not in any way sever the link with the war imagined, prepared for and sometimes fantasized about in the years prior to its outbreak.

Although Jean-Michel Steg refrains from judging the social actors of the time, beginning with the leaders at the highest echelons, many years after the fact, it is hardly unreasonable to conclude that our present weighs on the perspective he brings to bear on the elites of 1914, particularly military officials. Coming from the world of finance – in passing, it should be mentioned that the author's achievement here is proof that history is not the realm uniquely of professional historians – Steg was an inside observer of the global financial system's downfall in 2008, whose seriousness and eventual consequences constitute without a doubt a new 'strange defeat' of entire swathes of the Western elite, a collapse to be put on the same footing, perhaps, as the one that Marc Bloch branded with infamy in the book that took as its inspiration the May–June 1940 debacle and was written the summer of the same year.[5] From this perspective, it is instructive to read the pages devoted by the author to the extraordinary testimony given by Joffre – who is treated with considerable indulgence by Marc Bloch, himself a veteran of the 'Miracle of the Marne' – before the parliamentary commission of inquiry chaired by Maurice Viollette on 4 July 1919. Steg's discussion of this issue demonstrates once again that the questions we ask of the past are always drawn from those we ask about our own time. And these underlying interrogations are one of the great merits of this terse and sinewy book.

Stéphane Audoin-Rouzeau
EHESS

PREFACE

This book is, above all, a book about death, and more specifically violent death in the twentieth century.

As the first child born in France to a family who emigrated between the two wars, I do not have any familial ties to the experience of the First World War in my parents' adopted country. My interest in the unprecedented peak in mortality that occurred during the war's first battles comes from reading a seminal work in the field by Jay Winter, a Yale professor and one of the leading American specialists on this war to end all wars, *The Great War and the Shaping of the Twentieth Century*, a companion volume to a public television series, co-authored with Blaine Baggett.[6] Winter and Baggett's book includes a very extensive – and fascinating – collection of archival images. It was the caption to a photo showing French infantrymen crouched behind a mound of earth that set me thinking: '27,000 Frenchmen died on 22 August 1914, the bloodiest day in the country's military history.'[7] This simple statement aroused within me a whole host of questions, which I still find compelling today: did 27,000 men really die on that single day? Thus even before the Battle of the Marne? How many died at Verdun? At the Chemin des Dames? At Waterloo? At Agincourt? Where were these men killed? In just one battle or several? Under what circumstances? In artillery attacks? Under machine-gun fire? And so on. Maybe it is a legacy of my main career as a financier, but I am accustomed to examining heaps of figures to try to give them meaning, and records of military casualties are as open to analysis as any other type of data. So many deaths in a single day, without precedent or later equivalent in the history of France, cannot just be a statistical anomaly. It must mean something. But what? The aim of this book is at least to offer several possible avenues for answers.

I feel fortunate to have been born in Europe at the beginning of the second half of the twentieth century. I was thus saved the experience of what has been referred to as the 'hemoclysm' of its first half.[8] Growing up as I did, in peacetime, amid the prosperity of the 'thirty glorious years' in France, encouraged a tendency not to dwell too much on the many missing branches of my family tree and of those of others around me. So soon after emerging from catastrophe, the time was hardly ripe for remembrance, still less celebration. In my childhood and adolescent years, I nevertheless recognized, perhaps implicitly, that the two great wars and their totalitarian ideologies – Nazism and communism – had devastated the worlds of everyone I knew.

Having no interest, from either an emotional or an intellectual standpoint, in carrying on the family's medical tradition, and facilitated by a French university system still reeling from the revolutionary ideas of the 'sixty-eighters', I was able, without too much effort, to pursue a first cycle of studies, which made up in breadth for what it lacked in depth, oscillating from political science and related fields at Sciences

Po to economics at the Panthéon and history at the Sorbonne. Not drawn to any particular profession, like my classmates I drifted aimlessly, our serene confidence inspired by France's full-employment economy at the time, the culmination of three decades of growth.[9] A series of unlikely encounters, unexpected but beneficial for me, led me first to continue my studies in the United States, and then to a career in finance. Beginning in the early 1980s, the growing financialization of the world's economies, combined with the emergence of globalization, had turned on its head the industry I had entered in some ways by chance. In this field, my generation rode a thirty-year wave, which brought opportunities – to those lucky enough to find themselves in the right place at the right time – for professional and material successes far beyond what they could ever have imagined on the basis of their natural talents.

Intensely, and without a doubt excessively, focused on my career for many years, I still had a thirst for the study of history. In the years I had lived in the United States, my intellectual curiosity had been piqued by a field of historical knowledge and analysis that had been completely absent during my studies in France – that of war. When I was a student in Paris, Fernand Braudel and the Annales school, with roots in certain aspects of structuralism and Marxism, had an overriding influence on the study and teaching of history. All efforts were concentrated on the *longue durée* (the long term), structures and the masses. The study of short-lived dramatic events, and its obsession with chronology, seemed obsolete. As one facet of this pursuit, military history was considered the fiefdom of political conservatives. And both of these presumed defects were ascribed to the study of battles. Steeped in Anglo-Saxon pragmatism, American and British historians had preserved and continually revisited this field of study, enjoying a relatively plentiful – and certainly passionate – readership. On a personal level, I recall the excitement I felt the first time I read Victor Davis Hanson's *The Western Way of War*[10] or the works of John Keegan, the eminent British military historian, who died in 2012. The quest to shed light on topics such as the way in which the ancient Greek hoplite phalanx advanced in battle or the intense dread of bombardment experienced by modern infantrymen had begun to intrigue me.

Reading these works not only rekindled my intellectual interest in the field of history, but sparked a vague and nebulous yearning, both intensely conditional and deeply ambiguous, to take up the study of history once again at some point. Imprudently, I spoke of these wistful plans from time to time, when among my family or friends. It so happens that I have the great fortune to be married to a woman whose renowned pragmatism and effectiveness combine with a firm line when it comes to daydreaming and procrastination. One morning, she informed me that I would soon be fifty, and that she felt it was high time that I made good on what I said I would do... one day. To this end, she set up an appointment for me with a research director who had recently joined the faculty of the École des Hautes Études en Sciences Sociales (EHESS), concluding that he might be amenable to taking on a new student, even one as wanting as myself.

It was thus that, on a date agreed between him and my spouse, I found myself ringing the bell of Stéphane Audoin-Rouzeau, at that time already a widely reputed specialist on the First World War. In him, I discovered a genuine master, by which I mean someone who possesses immense knowledge, but also has the generosity necessary to pass on at least some of it. Added to this, 'S.A.R.' (as his students call him) is blessed with the natural indulgence and sense of humour required when burdened with such an unlikely, over-the-hill student. And this is why, for nearly ten years now, on two or three Mondays every month of the (far too short) university year, I have been taking advantage of the seniority acquired over time in my profession to attend EHESS seminars.

As it accepts only students intending to engage in research

(at least in principle), the EHESS operates under an unusual model, its curriculum not including any lecture courses. The programme of studies is structured around research seminars bringing together doctoral students and established researchers in the social sciences under the supervision of a research director. As I would soon realize, at these seminars one could also find, if authorized by the research director, a panoply of individuals from very different walks of life (physicians, military officers, clergymen, artists, business people, and so on) united by their shared intellectual interest in the seminar's theme. It is not overstating the case to say that 'the École', as its students and faculty call it, offers possibilities for intellectual development without equal in the world for anyone with a research interest in any area of the social sciences. Its offering covers a range of about a thousand themes – the number of seminars programmed over the university year.

For several years, I have thus had the privilege of participating as a regular attendee in two EHESS seminars, as well as the customary informal discussions afterwards in the cafes on the Boulevard Raspail. The first of these, led for many years now by Anne Rasmussen and Christophe Prochasson, is officially titled 'Historiographie de la Première Guerre mondiale' (Historiography of the First World War), but is referred to by everyone as the 'Séminaire Poilu', which perfectly captures its subject.[11] The second, conceived by Stéphane Audoin-Rouzeau and bearing the general title 'Anthropologie historique de la violence de guerre au XXème siècle' (Historical anthropology of war violence in the twentieth century), takes as its theme the sombre events at the heart of contemporary battles, whatever the place or circumstances. Cross-cutting in concept, this seminar thus focuses on the scientific investigation of actions, behaviour or situations in which our natural tendency as individuals is precisely to avoid exploring further: Thanatos works under a veil of modesty, providing just as effective cover as that of Eros.

A century after the events, the volume of research and published work on the First World War is impressive. It would be easy to conclude that, by now, everything has been said, written, analysed and surveyed. And yet, even on a personal and anecdotal level, I am astonished, for example, by how often friends of mine, upon learning of my interest in this period, tell me that they have in their possession notebooks, memoirs, letters or accounts left behind by a long-deceased ancestor. These sometimes passionate, and often moving, accounts at times bring to the surface the painful memory of familial tragedies with far-reaching and complex ramifications.

If I had thought that this investigation into war casualties would eventually depersonalize these many testimonies and accounts and anaesthetize me to them (in the way that, for an oncologist, clinical detachment combined with experience helps create distance between the practitioner and the patient's suffering), I could not have been more wrong. The more I worked on the circumstances behind the deaths, over a century ago, of these thousands of men, the more I was overcome by their humanity, making the writing even more difficult than it already was for me.

CHAPTER 1

AN UNKNOWN CATASTROPHE

On 22 August 1914, France experienced a military disaster of historic proportions. In the space of this single day, more than 27,000 French soldiers and officers lost their lives: a level of losses never seen before or since. And yet this human and military catastrophe has not left any trace in French collective memory. It has hardly attracted the attention of French historians either. This indifference, in turn, raises its own set of questions.

Such a high toll of casualties was completely without precedent and has never been equalled, even on the worst days of the Battle of Verdun and of the three battles fought along the Chemin des Dames. And although the French army sustained far greater losses at the Walloon villages of Rossignol, Saint-Vincent and Neufchâteau, those names do not resonate with the same impact as those of Agincourt and Waterloo.[12] These losses were sustained in a number of separate engagements and on several fronts, from Charleroi and the heights of the

Sambre to Longwy and Morhange in Lorraine and up again into the Vosges. These battles decimated indiscriminately both seasoned professional French colonial forces and reserve regiments, the latter having just arrived from the Nice and Marseilles depots. Moreover, they contributed to the annihilation of a good portion of the French intellectual elite in the first weeks of the war, famously including Charles Péguy, killed at the Battle of the Marne on 5 September, and Alain-Fournier, mortally wounded in action on 22 September, but also Ernest Renan's grandson, Ernest Psichari, killed while reconnoitring ahead of his troops, at Saint-Vincent in the Belgian Ardennes on 22 August.

Over the course of the entire war, the only day which, in terms of human losses, comes close to the bloodbath of 22 August 1914 is 1 July 1916, when British troops launched an attack on a ridge in the Somme, between Vimy and Bapaume, leaving 20,000 British dead by nightfall. Significantly, and in complete contrast with the lacunar amnesia on this subject in France, it would be difficult to find a British schoolchild not having at least a passing knowledge of that day's events, an awareness nurtured since the war and right up to the present day thanks to a constantly renewed flow of articles, books, films and television programmes.[13]

Quantitative information, however precise, cannot alone purport to elucidate fully any historical event, whatever the circumstances. Nevertheless, when this event is a war, it cannot begin to be understood without first completing the macabre accounting of losses. Deaths are a key fact in any war. It is not possible to speak of one without the other and a number of fundamental points must be addressed: when? How many? How? Where? Even before attempting to answer the crucial question: why?

The profound effects on American society of the Vietnam War, which lasted from 1959 to 1975, only really began to be healed with the completion in 1982 of the polished black granite memorial in Washington DC referred to familiarly as 'the Wall', inscribed with the names of the more than 58,000 men and women who gave their lives during that conflict or who remain missing. This statistic needs to be set against the population of the United States during this period, which was about 200 million. Thus the France of 1914, with its 39 million inhabitants, lost in a single day nearly half of the total number of American soldiers killed in sixteen years of conflict in Vietnam, and more than twice that number over five days of fighting in the Belgian Ardennes. It is also worth noting that French casualties that day were virtually equivalent to the number of French killed during the entire Algerian War, from 1954 to 1962.

Between August 1914 and November 1918, 1.4 million French soldiers were killed; thus nearly 900 lives were lost per day on average in about 1,560 days of fighting. This deadly disaster therefore reached a high point, paradoxically – if it is in fact a paradox – at the *very start* of the conflict. Does this statistical oddity reflect some sort of epiphenomenon? Or is it the result of bad, or simply unfortunate, individual and collective tactical, strategic or organizational choices?

An examination of First World War mortality data by nationality (see Table 1) reveals other surprising facts. Apart from the exceptional level of casualties seen in the war's Balkan theatre,[14] virtually unknown today in Western Europe, one is struck immediately by the relatively limited German losses compared to those suffered by their adversaries. On the Western Front, despite the absence of any decisive battle for either side, German losses for the entire duration of the war amounted overall to fewer than half of Allied losses.[15] Here we thus need to note the inversion of the traditional rule according to which the human losses of the vanquished are generally several times greater than those of the victors. In the autumn of 1918, the German army, enfeebled by its unsuccessful and bloody offensives during the spring of the same year, and its numbers dwindling, beat a swift retreat on all fronts. This forced withdrawal, combined with the collapse of its domestic economy and the fall of its monarchy, was to compel Germany to seek an armistice without having been defeated in any decisive battle.[16] It is true that the strategies of armies on either side of the line were at cross-purposes. In fact, throughout most of the conflict, the Western Front maintained exceptional stability. Beginning with the stabilization of positions following the First Battle of the Marne, the line separating opposing armies from the beaches along the English Channel to the Swiss border did not vary anywhere by more than thirty kilometres, until the German offensive in the spring of 1918. With the exception of the first six weeks of the war, the Verdun offensive in February 1916 and that of March–July 1918, the German armies essentially remained in a defensive posture. On the other hand, the Allied armies were constantly in search of a decisive opening on the Western Front, without ever succeeding. Figures for the number killed each year reveal that 1915 was the war's bloodiest for the French army. Mortality rates fell in 1916 as against 1915, then again in 1917 compared to 1916. Deaths rose again in 1918, under the dual impact of the return to a 'war of movement' and the epidemic of Spanish influenza. If we examine the trend in the number of soldiers killed on a monthly basis, we note that the first months of the war were by far the bloodiest (see Table 2), since in just five months of a war that would last for fifty-two, nearly a quarter of all French casualties were recorded. Over the war's duration, the belligerents seemed to have benefited from experience, allowing them to persevere in an extended conflict by gradually limiting their relative losses, mainly by stationing their men in trenches and curtailing as much as possible the length of their attacks or those exposing troops to direct enemy fire. And even under these conditions, losses were recorded at levels unimaginable at the beginning of the war.

With this first great war of the twentieth century, firepower attained truly industrial proportions, meaning that no one could remain standing on the battlefield, even for an instant, without endangering his life. A 'war of movement' thus constitutes a much more deadly environment than a 'war of positions', despite the latter's extreme level of discomfort for the soldiers. Decimating troops well protected by trenches requires a great deal of shelling.[17] The decision to carry out an offensive is a choice made in the knowledge that it will mean the sacrifice of one's own troops, justified (or not) by the quest for a decisive opening.

The defensive posture thus prevailed due to the confluence of two strong trends, one technological and the other operational, leading to a significant rise in casualties in wars fought by European armies. The second half of the nineteenth century saw an unprecedented increase in the pace of technical progress. Thus, although between Fontenoy (1745) and Waterloo (1815) neither weaponry nor battle tactics in use by European armies was the focus of any major changes, in the following hundred years a complete transformation was accomplished. Anyone over sixty in 1914 had, since his or her birth, lived to see the invention and development of spark-ignition engines, steamships, railways, electric motors, automobiles, aeroplanes, submarines, electric light bulbs, telegraphs, telephones and more. Scientific, technical, technological and industrial development hardly neglected the fields of war and weaponry, especially beginning in the 1880s. Progress made in the chemistry of explosives (high explosives, smokeless powders, high-velocity ammunition) combined with achievements in precision metallurgy and mechanics. These advances enabled the development of weapons able to fire rounds with an enhanced capacity for destruction across ever greater distances, with more accuracy, at increasingly rapid intervals. Industrialization led to the production of these weapons in ever larger quantities. These developments would intensify the firepower of belligerents to such a degree that it was no longer possible to keep troops on the battlefield, which thus needed to be emptied of any visible human presence.

With both France and Germany's armies comprising several million infantrymen, small arms saw the most significant fundamental change. Rifles used by French troops in the Revolutionary and Napoleonic wars could fire three spherical balls per minute, provided they were handled by very experienced soldiers. Models like the Lebel 86/93 and the Mauser 98 were able to fire more than twenty shots per minute and over long distances. By the end of the nineteenth century, with the availability of machine guns able to fire a minimum of 400 rounds per minute, it was no longer well advised to have foot soldiers circulating freely over open terrain. These new weapons were to bring about a complete transformation in the behaviour of individuals on the battlefield.

But technical progress cannot alone explain the nearly exponential growth in destructive military capacity. For the greatest possible effectiveness, this rise in capacity needed to be accompanied by a strengthened social organization. At the declaration of war on 2 August 1914, being able to take an individual, very often a farmer, from Béarn, Brittany or the Dauphiné, and transform him in less than three weeks, along with several million of his fellow countrymen, into a fully armed and equipped soldier advancing in formation on the country's north-eastern borderlands, required far more than the invention of the railway. It demanded a system of power: registration, enrolment, classification by the recruitment board, training, creation of depots, sophisticated logistics for transmission and transport, communications and administration, and so on – components that had been put in place gradually since the start of the modern era, integrated and perfected under the Third Republic in France, building on the Napoleonic heritage. It was thus that, in August 1914, two armies of unprecedented size (more than a million men each on the Western Front), abundantly equipped with the most destructive munitions ever manufactured to date, would meet each other head on.

Armies and their staff officers had been preparing for this day over the forty-three previous years, since the Franco-Prussian War of 1870–1. Each according to its history, its traditions and the ideology of its elites, sought to anticipate the change in military tactics and organization made necessary by the Industrial Revolution.

Officers examined the battle history of the Russo-Japanese War of 1904–5 from top to bottom and, to a lesser extent, the conflict between the Boers and the British army (1899–1902) as well as the Balkan Wars of 1912–13, which saw the first massive commitments of troops equipped with modern firepower. Significantly, conclusions drawn and observations of identical facts often diverged considerably on either side of the Rhine, especially in terms of the organization of command and doctrine. Those responsible for the French armed forces would debate at great length the primacy of attacking over defending, encapsulated in the concept known as *offensive à outrance*, or 'all-out offensive', its presumed suitability to the French natural character, and whether or not it was appropriate given advances in and the proliferation of firepower. The two conferences for staff officers given in 1911 by the French lieutenant colonel and military theorist Louis Loyzeau de Grandmaison, who had founded the Centre des Hautes Études Militaires (CHEM), laid down this doctrine, under which the French army had to maintain its will to conquer (what the Italians famously called the *furia francese*), which had always (with the notable exception of the 1870 defeat) allowed it to triumph over troops from the other side of the Rhine, typically known to be better equipped and more disciplined. These choices, both explicit and implicit, would find bloody corroboration from the very first battles of the second half of August 1914, first in Alsace and then in Lorraine, and then simultaneously in the western and central areas of the Belgian Ardennes.

Even if there was a surfeit of courage on the French side, it was not, for the most part, because French soldiers in blue coats and bright-red trousers made heroic, flag-waving assaults, responding to orders relayed by bugle calls, that the country's army was routed so thoroughly, although this fact has been put out of mind ever since. Mainly, it was due to the dense and accurate rifle fire laid down by German troops who were better trained, better commanded in battle, deployed more rapidly, and more autonomous and freer in their movements; and who took by surprise French troops who were handicapped by a command system as hierarchical as it was rigid, and stupefied to see themselves decimated before even realizing that the battle had begun. The very magnitude of the carnage inflicted during the fighting on 22 August, as well as the imperfect means of communication and control, initially surprised the command personnel, French as well as German, to the point of paralysing them for a time. The French hierarchy had great difficulty passing the reports on the extent of the catastrophe from rank to rank, without understating the events. Although its troops remained the masters of the terrain on the evening of 22 August, the German command greeted the figures of its own losses (albeit less than half as extensive as those of the French forces) with utter disbelief. Struck with the extent of its casualties, the German command very logically wondered if it had really emerged victorious from the day's battles. Hence its hesitation at continuing the campaign, especially as the surviving troops were exhausted and since so many of the subalterns and non-commissioned officers (who played a vital role in German tactical plans) were among the victims. This respite allowed the French troops to retreat, in a relatively organized fashion, to the Marne, and thus contributed to the slowdown that prevented the First World War from playing out as planned by the staff officers, who had anticipated that it would certainly be bloody, with many casualties, but short.

Discussions of the disastrous events of the Battle of the Frontiers were initiated by Joseph Joffre, the French commander-in-chief, while the fighting was still under way. Already on 21 August, upon hearing news of the French failure to advance in Lorraine, at a time when he was still unaware of the catastrophic developments in the Belgian Ardennes, Joffre phoned Adolphe Messimy, the war minister, and offered his analysis in the following terms: 'The offensive in Lorraine got off to a great start. But this momentum was abruptly cut short by either individual or collective failings, which led to a general retreat and cost us very heavy losses [...] I am initiating court-martial proceedings.' The immediate consequences, from late August, were brutal at every level, except that of the chief of staff: the replacement of Messimy as war minister with Alexandre Millerand, the exile of disgraced generals to Limoges[18] (the site of the military headquarters for the Centre Region), and above all the handing down of the ultimate penalty by courts martial and other special jurisdiction court hearings. The first 'official' firing-squad victim by decision of a special jurisdiction court was a commanding officer, the battalion leader Wolff (of the 37th Colonial Infantry Regiment's fourth battalion[19]), executed on 1 September for having attempted to surrender his troops to enemy forces on 25 August.[20]

The fact that the war continued apace created an environment hardly conducive to deeper discussions about responsibilities for such high initial human losses. However, after the war had ended, and especially in the 1920s, a large number of first-hand accounts emerged, from the lowliest foot soldiers to subalterns and even lieutenant generals (see Appendix 2 for excerpts from the account provided by General Fernand de Langle de Cary, commander of the Fourth Army). Many explanations for the disaster were offered, from individual command inadequacies to collective failures by troops. For example, the blame for the routing of the Second Army in Lorraine was frequently ascribed to its XV Corps, consisting of Provençal reservists, (wrongly) accused of deserting as a group.[21] Those bearing witness often spoke of the circumstances of war as being as unpredictable as they were unfortunate: for example, the fog that masked the German troops as they took up positions in the Belgian Ardennes in the early hours of 22 August. Once the war was over, many voices rose to find fault with the staff officers, and Joffre in particular, going so far as to create a French version of the concise phrase popularly used to lambaste British generals for having sent so many brave soldiers to their deaths: *'Des lions menés par des ânes'* (lions led by donkeys).[22]

Apropos or not, the rush to attribute the disaster to inadequacies at the level of high command presented the problem, for the political and military elites, of dividing the nation and its army by discrediting, after the fact, decorated military leaders presumed to have led French armies to victory in the best way possible.

It was thus that a consensus emerged in France after the war explaining the setbacks of the first weeks as being the result of an overall mindset that was valiant but inappropriate – that of the *offensive à outrance* (all-out offensive) – without putting any particular emphasis on the level of losses. The first explanation for these initial setbacks and catastrophic losses automatically brought to mind the image of a rushing, heroic and mad charge, without cover of artillery, as soon as the enemy became visible. No matter that direct testimony as well as regimental reports, both German and French, tended to challenge this explanation: it had the merit of being more satisfying for the military elites, both institutionally and from a moral standpoint, than a close analysis of their own failings and inadequacies. Moreover, most of the theorists of the all-out offensive had obligingly got themselves killed at the front, as was the case for Louis Loyzeau de Grandmaison, thus simplifying the debate. This led to the emergence, between the two world wars, of a new French military doctrine, one that was this time resolutely defensive, and which quite patently turned its back on the supposed mistakes of the earlier era. But it unfortunately retained all of the rigidity and deficiencies that had largely helped bring about the previous disaster and would contribute to the following one.

The primary objective of this work is to relate simple facts: the events of that catastrophic day, which are well known among historians but hardly at all to the wider public. Numerous and varied sources are available: regimental and divisional newsletters, accounts by French or German survivors, works by historians on the Battle of the Frontiers, and so on. What exactly happened that day, from a military perspective, to result in such carnage?

But this book also aims to find elements that might help explain such a rise in battle mortality numbers. We need to consider the strategic, tactical, technical, organizational, not to mention political and cultural, factors that brought about this change.

One last point: French readers in particular are invited to engage in an exercise of memory. How did a defeat so catastrophic (it is difficult to describe it in any other way) vanish so completely from collective memory? Especially given the fact that this period of history is not otherwise excluded from national memory in France. The sacrifices of the thousands of men who died that day do not deserve to be forgotten.

CHAPTER 2

THE BATTLE OF ROSSIGNOL: AN HOUR-BY-HOUR RECONSTRUCTION

6.30 A.M.: PUSHING FORWARD THROUGH FOG

On the early morning of 22 August 1914, the advance guard of the French 3rd Colonial Infantry Division pushes slowly northward along the narrow route through the Belgian Ardennes forest in the direction of the village of Rossignol. Leaving the tiny hamlet of Saint-Vincent near the Belgian border, they cross the Semois, a tributary of the Meuse, at the Mesnil–Breuvanne bridge. In this southernmost province of Belgium adjacent to the Grand Duchy of Luxembourg, the terrain is difficult – wooded, undulating, and dotted with ponds and marshes. Advancing off-road is not an easy task, especially for the horse-drawn artillery and supply wagon. Heavy rains the previous day have left the ground very wet, and this combined with the thick August heat is making the task harder still: a dense fog covers the countryside, partially concealing the troops.

Although the German forces, following the Schlieffen Plan (see Map 1), had invaded Belgium from the east on 2 August, this is the first time that French forces are crossing in large numbers into Belgian territory in support of the nation's new ally. By doing so, they are carrying the battle beyond their own borders, over terrain that they have not been able to reconnoitre beforehand. Two French armies, the Fifth, under its commander General Charles Lanrezac, holding the western edge of the line near Charleroi and Namur, and the Fourth, led by General de Langle de Cary in the Ardennes (for which the Colonial Corps serves as the right flank), are thus destined to go up against the German forces. Prior to this encounter, after first breaking through deeply from east to west in Belgium, the Germans have made use of their most powerful land weapons either to destroy or to force the surrender of all twelve forts ringing the city of Liège, subsequently managing to capture Brussels without resistance on 20 August, marching through and heading further southward.

Despite their fatigue, the French colonial troops remain energized. Apart from exchanges of fire with cavalry out on a reconnoitring mission, the French have not fought with the Germans since leaving Bar-le-Duc, in Lorraine, three days earlier. However, on the previous day, due to a number of logistical blunders, the men and their officers had been taken on an exhausting series of ineffective marches and counter-marches. Having thus marched for nearly twenty hours on 21 August, before being billeted around midnight, the men find themselves setting off again at dawn. No hot meals have been served, not even a breakfast at first light. As for the officers, they have been getting by with perhaps two to three hours sleep a night at most for the past three days.

The colonial infantry corps to which the 3rd Colonial Division belongs is an elite unit made up not of men from the French colonies but of professional soldiers, most of whom have already served in Africa or Indochina. This is due to the fact that sending draftees overseas is prohibited under French law. In peacetime, the 3rd Colonial Division is based in Brest, where reservists and conscripts had begun to arrive in early August. Many of the reservists are former Colonial Corps members: more than 75 per cent of the troops in this division are professional soldiers who have already seen action. But these soldiers have never – not in Tonkin, equatorial Africa, Madagascar or the Rif – had to face artillery barrages and dense rifle fire like those of a modern European army. No matter how many battles they have seen, they are thus moving into an entirely new realm of experience, one for which they are ill prepared.

French staff officers are not expecting to see fighting this day. The aim is to push rapidly northward in order to reach the town of Neufchâteau, about thirty kilometres from the border. This is where they think their forces will encounter the Germans and wage battle over the following days. Dated the morning of 22 August, the wire sent by the Colonial Corps's general staff is clear:

> Colonial Corps has only run across patrols from the German 3rd and 8th Cavalry Divisions. These skeletal German forces were routed on 17th and 18th [August] by our own cavalry.

Unfortunately, this information is incorrect. In fact, this same day the Colonial Corps is to run up against the German Third Army's VI Corps, and in particular its 21st and 22nd Infantry Divisions, which had arrived at Neufchâteau the day before. The poorly coordinated soldiers of the French 3rd Colonial Infantry Division quickly lose the advantage in this imprudently fought battle, suffering a series of setbacks over the course of the day. The cumulative effect of these reversals will be the near destruction of these forces.

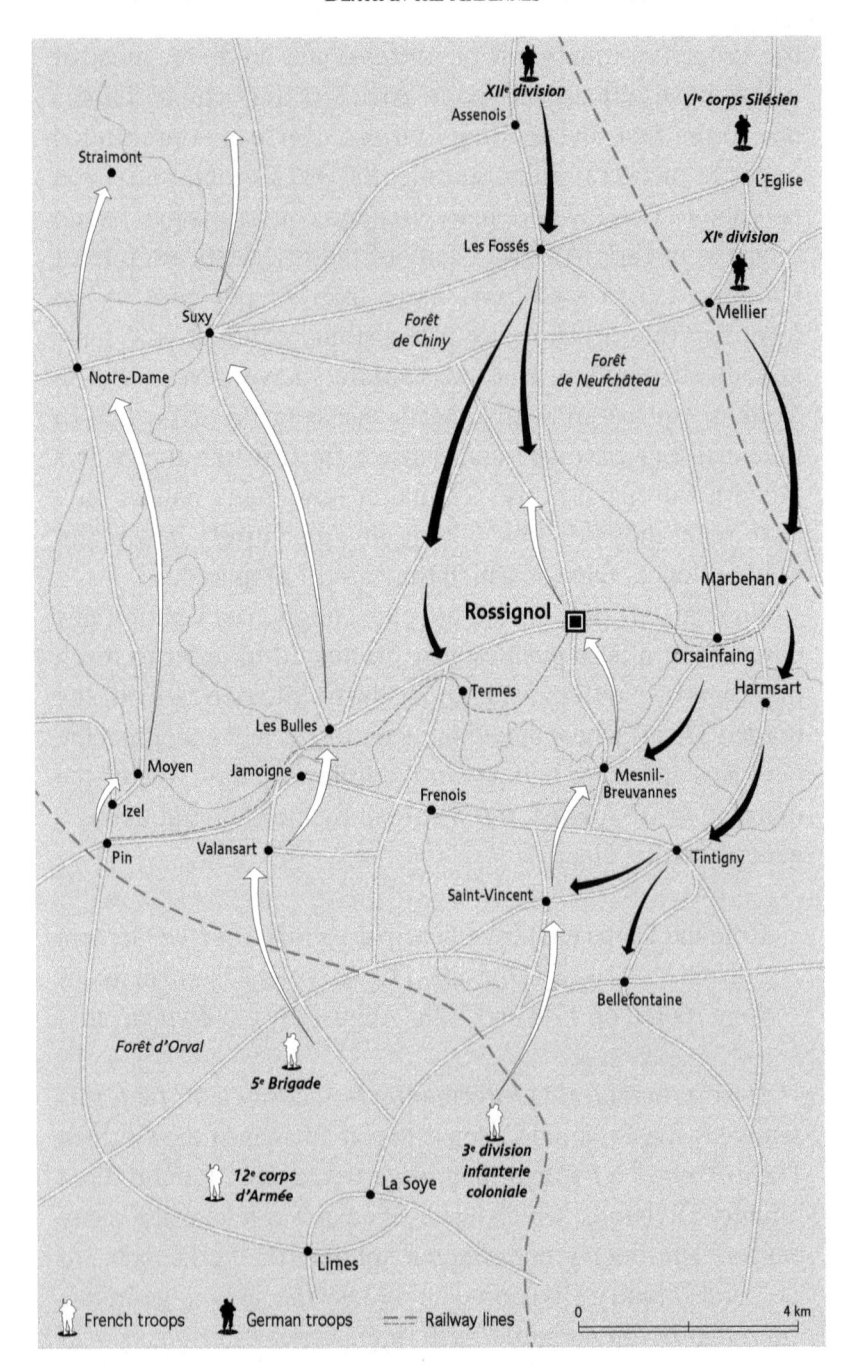

6.30 a.m.: Beginning of operations

7 A.M.: First Contact with the Germans

The French columns are compelled to advance along a narrow country lane, resulting in a formation more than ten kilometres long. This formation consists of two brigades, the First and the Third, each composed of two colonial infantry regiments (the 1st and 2nd Colonial Infantry Regiments forming the First Brigade and the 3rd and 7th Colonial Infantry Regiments forming the Second Brigade), thus a total of nearly 20,000 men. The 1st Colonial Regiment serves as the 3rd Colonial Division's advance guard, along with the 2nd Colonial Corps Artillery Regiment, the divisional artillery. It is preceded by a cavalry unit, the Sixth Dragoons, who reach Rossignol first. The rearguard (the 7th Colonial Infantry Regiment and the 3rd Colonial Corps Artillery Regiment together with a Chasseurs d'Afrique regiment) is still in Saint-Vincent and has yet to cross the Mesnil–Breuvanne bridge.

The French dragoons thus enter Rossignol and exchange shots with a patrol of German Uhlans they discover upon arriving, whom they push back to the northern edge of the village. The German cavalry patrol falls back to the dense forest extending between Rossignol and Neufchâteau. The dragoons try to follow them, but are repelled at the edge of the forest by intense fire. In their report, they speak of meeting German troops well entrenched in the forest.

With the fog clearing under the heat of the sun, the Germans, until then as unaware of the positions taken up by the French as the French had been of their own, now begin to gain a pretty clear idea of the numbers, organization and whereabouts of the opposing troops. In contrast, the French, in the absence of effective reconnaissance or adequate and timely transmission of information through the division's hierarchy, are still convinced that there is only a smattering of troops in their path. A fundamental tactical advantage has therefore just been acquired by the opposing forces. The latter will hold on to this advantage throughout the entire day, with the French continually surprised by the attacks of their German counterparts, whose numbers and position remain a complete mystery to them.

Upon his arrival at Rossignol, General Charles Montignault, the commander of the First Brigade (the 1st and 2nd Colonial Infantry Regiments), must choose between entering the forest or playing for time by running reconnaissance missions. On the one hand, it is clear that the terrain is particularly hostile to the progression of the French troops: a single, narrow route crossing a dense forest, itself surrounded by ponds and marshes, making it impossible to circumvent. On the other hand, he has received perfectly clear and unambiguous instructions from the general staff: the thirty-three kilometres between the starting positions of the colonial troops and Neufchâteau must be covered in less than five hours, so as to allow for the regrouping of troops, beginning at 11 a.m., in order to attack the Germans over the following days.

Montignault quickly makes his choice: in light of the information received from the Colonial Corps's general staff, he decides that the shots heard can only be those fired by cavalry on individual reconnaissance missions. Montignault thus feels the moment is ripe to push forward with conviction and cross the forest quickly. He therefore orders the 1st Colonial Infantry Regiment's three battalions into the woods, one after the other, beginning with the second battalion. But the artillery regiment, unable to take up position on the narrow route, or for that matter to manoeuvre on its banks, is sent back to the rear in the direction of Rossignol.

In fact, the German troops already occupy Neufchâteau, having arrived in this village the previous night. They also did not expect to encounter their adversaries at this early stage, but the morning reconnaissance missions of the Uhlans (and the lifting of the fog) have given them a tactical advantage, which they will successfully exploit to the full. In contrast to the French, the Germans quickly adapt their formation to the new circumstances. Like their adversaries, they are advancing in columns several kilometres in length. But, unlike them, the Germans have access to the appropriate information and make the tactical decision to establish a defensive line, putting it in place rapidly.

To prevent the French from advancing further northward, the local German commanders have organized defences in the bushes and shrubs of the forest of Neufchâteau so as to rake the only route passing through these woods with machine-gun fire. At the same time, they have set up their field artillery at positions north-west and north-east of Rossignol in order to inflict the largest number of casualties among the French troops. The latter continue to advance, still unaware that they are about to run up against Germany forces now organized in defensive positions with their entire firepower available.

It is this defensive line, put in place quickly but deadly in its efficiency, that the soldiers of the 1st Colonial Infantry Regiment's second battalion, commanded by Lieutenant Colonel Vitard, will be the first to encounter. This assault by French soldiers against machine-gun crews and riflemen protected by trenches, even hastily dug ones, will be delivered the fate handed down to every endeavour of this type attempted over the course of the First World War: utter failure and slaughter of the attacking forces, whatever their drive and courage. Cut down by machine-gun fire while advancing on the route, the French soldiers of the 1st Colonial Regiment's second battalion are no more able to make headway along the marshy banks or in the surrounding brush, where they remain exposed without being able to take cover from the dense and precise rifle fire laid down by the German soldiers.

After several minutes of slaughter, the first wounded soldiers begin to emerge from the woods to inform Vitard of this unexpected resistance. But the French commander's reaction is identical to the one that will be seen at the various battle sites in the Ardennes whenever enemy opposition makes its presence known: he calls for an immediate reinforced attack.

The 1st Colonial Regiment thus brings its remaining resources to bear (first and third battalions) to try to force its way past the enemy.[23] The men mount the charge, officers at the helm, and run up against the same wall of fire as their predecessors, with even more drastic results than during the first assault. In the space of just a few minutes, the entire regiment is massacred, its three battalion leaders killed in front of their men, along with most of the other officers.

8.45 A.M.: HESITATIONS BY THE FRENCH GENERAL STAFF

The 3rd Colonial Infantry Division's general staff, still advancing with most of the troops on the road to Rossignol, hears the heavy rifle fire and begins to see the wounded, in increasing numbers, strewn along the road. Dispatch riders return with the initial reports on the number of losses, as yet imprecise, but rising steadily. Then the first superior officers begin to appear. Montignault emerges, lamenting the death of his staff officer, cut down before his eyes. He is followed by Vitard, a battle-hardened Indochina veteran, his hands gravely wounded, who delivers a conclusive report: 'We were lured into an ambush!'[24]

At this, the officers begin to debate the matter intensely. Moreau, the 3rd Colonial Division's principal staff officer, suggests to its commander General Léon Raffenel that the troops stop advancing towards Rossignol and that patrols be sent to reconnoitre the German positions as well as the extent and depth of the front over which they are deployed. All in attendance are struck by Raffenel's growing state of agitation when he seems to falter for a moment before responding in jest, 'Hmph, you and your fronts! Go ahead and pull the other one!'[25] And he gives the order to move the 2nd Colonial Infantry Regiment forward.

So it is now this regiment's turn to rush into the forest of Neufchâteau, thereby earning the sad distinction of being the regiment suffering the day's highest toll of losses, notably including the annihilation of nearly all its officers. In less than two hours, with its two elite infantry regiments wiped out, the 3rd Colonial Division finds itself facing losses of colossal proportions, the total corresponding to more than a third of its combat capacity, and without its commanders ever understanding the nature of the battle to which they had committed their forces.

10 A.M.: GERMAN ARTILLERY BATTERIES ENTER INTO ACTION

This is the moment when, from its positions further east, the German artillery begins shelling the French positions on the road, in Rossignol itself and on the Mesnil–Breuvanne bridge. This is the bridge that is to be used by the remainder of Colonial Corps, in particular the 2nd Colonial Infantry Division, who are supposed to provide cover for the 3rd Colonial Infantry Division. Made impassable, the bridge is quickly destroyed, preventing the arrival of reinforcements at Rossignol. Deployed in reserve on the other bank of the Semois, the 2nd Colonial Division is thus not able to come to the aid of its brothers in arms (thus avoiding probable annihilation and preserving their numbers for future battles, during the retreat to the Marne).

Completely disorganized, the division's artillery tries to take a stand to the south of Rossignol, but it is already under enemy fire. From the heights where they have been able to gain a foothold, calmly and collectedly, over the last two hours, the German artillerymen are able to observe the French troops, who return fire blindly. Beginning at this point and until the end of the day, the French troops will have to contend with an uninterrupted deluge of artillery. The complete destruction by German fire of the colonial troops, already weakened by the successive attacks in the forest of Neufchâteau, now begins in earnest. Since early in the morning, the staggered deployment of troops along the route, the absence of systematic communication between the units and the weakness of the division command have made coordination difficult. As soon as the 3rd Colonial Division finds itself under German artillery fire, it is rapidly engulfed by its own disorganization.

The first consequence of the German shelling is to hasten the nervous breakdown of Raffenel, the division commander, clearly already very shaken by the development of a situation entirely slipping from his grasp, thus leaving his staff rudderless. Raffenel's adjutant Moreau describes the scene with a cruelty certainly motivated by the intense bitterness and deep resentment for a period of captivity that will begin the next day, from which he will never recover:[26]

> Ever since learning of the enemy shelling of the Mesnil–Breuvanne bridge and Saint-Vincent, the general seems stricken and disturbed. He remains as clueless as before that his command ought to be better organized and clearly lacks any idea of how this might be done. He continues to act as if he were alone, making no distinction in his mind between himself and his general staff, his general staff and his escort, the observation post and the weapons post, his decisions and their implementation. But now there's been a new development: his face is furrowed in gloomy concentration and he's unable to sit still. He seems to be looking for someone or something without knowing whom or what.[27]

Thus, by the end of the morning the commander of the French troops succumbs to a nervous collapse, without being replaced. Raffenel's decline will worsen throughout the day, as his deep melancholy increasingly gains the upper hand over

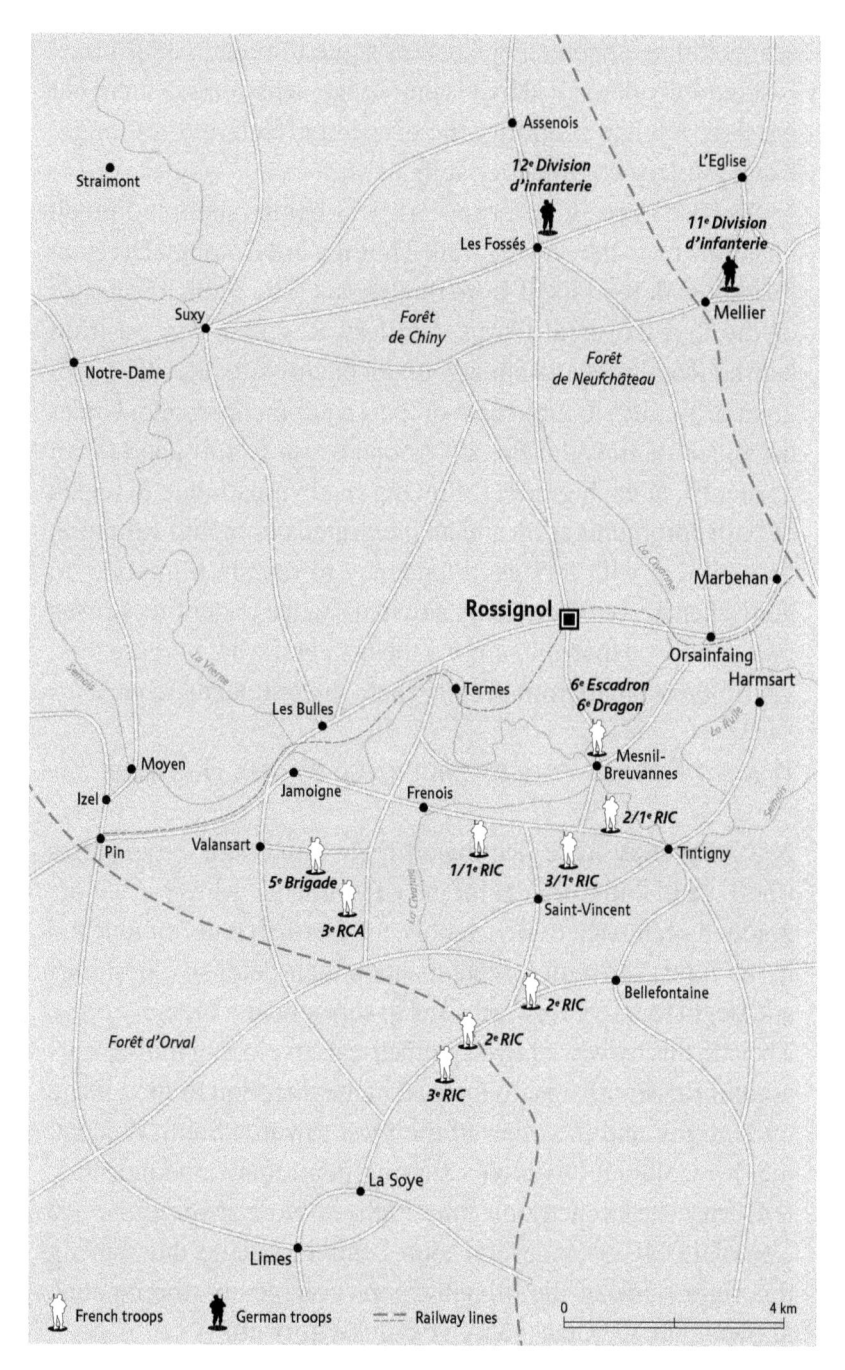

The Battle of Rossignol: An Hour-by-Hour Reconstruction

10 a.m.: Engagement of French troops against the Germans

any lingering bouts of hyperactive mania. His condition, which seems to have been an episode of acute traumatic delirium,[28] is accurately described by his entourage, who remain lucid but passive. By late morning, the division effectively no longer has a military commander at its helm.

At 10.30 a.m., the German artillery begins shelling French positions from the west as well. Thus the 3rd Colonial Division must now defend itself from three sides. The French batteries of the 2nd Colonial Corps Artillery Regiment, in position behind Rossignol and already under enemy fire, then try (with great difficulty) to turn some of their equipment around. Under the blaze of fire, the French troops begin to fall apart, with each unit, at each grade, following its own path due to a lack of both communication and an integrated command structure. And all this with a dogged tendency to remain immobile, to hold a heroic, but regrettably suicidal, stance under fire. Losses rise steadily, especially among the officers, who increase their visibility in an attempt to rally their shell-shocked troops.

11 A.M.: FRENCH FORCES ENCIRCLED BY THE GERMANS

Now that they have decimated their immediate adversaries (the 1st and 2nd Colonial Infantry Regiments, whose survivors gradually fall back to Rossignol), the German units entrenched in the forest of Neufchâteau abandon their defensive positions and begin to move forward so as to surround the French troops. They do this by way of two symmetrical enveloping movements around Rossignol, one to the east in the direction of the village of Tintigny and the other to the west towards Saint-Vincent, the 3rd Colonial Division's starting point that same morning. II Corps, the French unit that ought to have covered the 3rd Colonial Division, is several hours behind schedule, thus leaving this right flank of the French troops completely unprotected, allowing the Germans to move quickly forward.

Moreover, the Mesnil–Breuvanne bridge can no longer be

used to route reinforcements. Only the first of the 3rd Colonial Infantry Regiment's three battalions has managed to cross the bridge under fire. In any event, the remainder of the rearguard, with the 7th Colonial Infantry Regiment, the 3rd Colonial Corps Artillery Regiment and a battalion of the Chasseurs d'Afrique, will need to move rapidly into position between Saint-Vincent and Breuvanne to confront the German troops in the process of encircling Rossignol. To the north of the bridge, what remains of the units defeated in the forest of Neufchâteau and of those caught by the German counter-offensive on the route to Rossignol join together within the village and attempt, under intense shelling, to organize a defensive line.

However, as the German units seeking to surround them make their steady advance, the French units, their lack of coordination steadily worsening while their isolation increases, find themselves exposed not only to artillery barrages, but to rifle fire from German soldiers moving forward. Casualties rise, particularly among the officers. No one is left who might organize a retreat of a few kilometres in order to escape the encircling manoeuvre and the resulting decimation. Here and there, a surviving senior officer, or even a subaltern or non-commissioned officer, orders and leads a bayonet attack to try to loosen the enemy's grip. But these desperate attacks serve only to raise the number of casualties. Moreover, the attacks are often thwarted by rows of barbed-wire fencing, frequently encountered in this pasture-rich region.

Not a single officer steps up to organize and command a retreat beyond the river, which would clearly be the only rational military solution to the trap ensnaring the colonial troops.

Why have no orders been received from the commanders at the helm of an army known to follow hierarchical principles scrupulously (much more so than their German counterparts)? Is it because of a battle ethos (the cult of the offensive), internalized by every French officer from the very start of their training? Or have they succumbed to physical, mental and emotional paralysis under the German barrage? A bit of both, perhaps. In any event, not even the slightest initiative along these lines will be taken, up to the moment when the defeat is made inescapably apparent by the sight of troops gradually bled dry after several hours of exposure to running fire in open fields.

2 P.M.: FINAL ASSAULT BY THE GERMANS

The afternoon plays out in prolonged agony for the 3rd Colonial Infantry Division, suffering from a lack of effective command. At around 3.30 p.m., General Raffenel, completely abulic by this time, abandons the staff headquarters near Rossignol and is not heard from again. His body will only be found the next day, with no certainty as to whether he had died by his own hand or under enemy fire. Communications with the Colonial Corps's general staff, deficient at best all morning long, have now broken down completely. In any case, the 3rd Colonial Division can no longer count on help from anyone. The units on its right flank (II Corps) and on its left flank (Colonial Corps's Fifth Brigade), whose advance has not been coordinated with its own, are dealing with serious attacks from German units and are unable to come to their aid. The 3rd Colonial Division is now but a patchwork of disparate groups, gradually encircled in Rossignol first, and soon at Saint-Vincent and Breuvanne as well. These groups bring together fragments of various units, supplemented by individuals separated from their original units during the course of the battle.

The artillerymen, still contending with shelling from enemy batteries, start concentrating their firepower on targets directly in their sights: the lines of German foot soldiers advancing from the north, south and west towards the French positions. These attacks are not entirely in vain, provoking heavy losses among the assailants, who have left the protection of their defensive line and now move forward entirely exposed. The German survivors of this encounter will later wreak their vengeance on the civilian population of Rossignol.[29] The French artillerymen hold their positions, and die defending them. Among them, killed while reconnoitring in front of his troops, is the grandson of the scholar Ernest Renan, Lieutenant Psichari, himself a Saint-Cyr graduate and writer impregnated with mysticism, whose emblematic work *L'appel des armes* was a great literary success just before the war.[30] With only one among its forty officers surviving the carnage, the 2nd Colonial Corps Artillery Regiment is dispersed. It would not be re-established until 1917.

Paul Failin, a bugle corporal in the 3rd Colonial Infantry Regiment, left for dead that evening on the battlefield, speaks of the battle's last moments in the following terms:

> What a massacre! The route is a thick jumble of wagons, dead or wounded horses, fallen soldiers and felled trees. Further trees or branches keep being added to this pile. In the ditch, I spot the lifeless body of my artillery driver, his mouth covered in a pink foam. An ambulance is filled with the wounded – howling, whimpering and moaning with pain – many eased of further suffering by all the projectiles raining down from all sides.
>
> Seated, his back resting on the wheel, the medical officer, a red blotch on his chest, seems to be longing for death.
>
> I stop for an instant behind a gun aimed by the lieutenant himself at the infantry lines a short distance away. 'Don't stay there,' he barks at me, 'you'll lose a leg!' Sure enough, the cartridge heads are coming towards my feet. With each cannon blast, it's as if my head is being blown off. A young artilleryman, on his knees near his gun, rains rifle fire down on the men advancing on our position. 'C'mon guys, let's use up our last rounds!' he says.[31]
>
> A group of about a hundred men arrives from Rossignol, led by a quartermaster. 'We'll charge at them with bayonets!' he announces. They run to the left, in the direction of

Death in the Ardennes

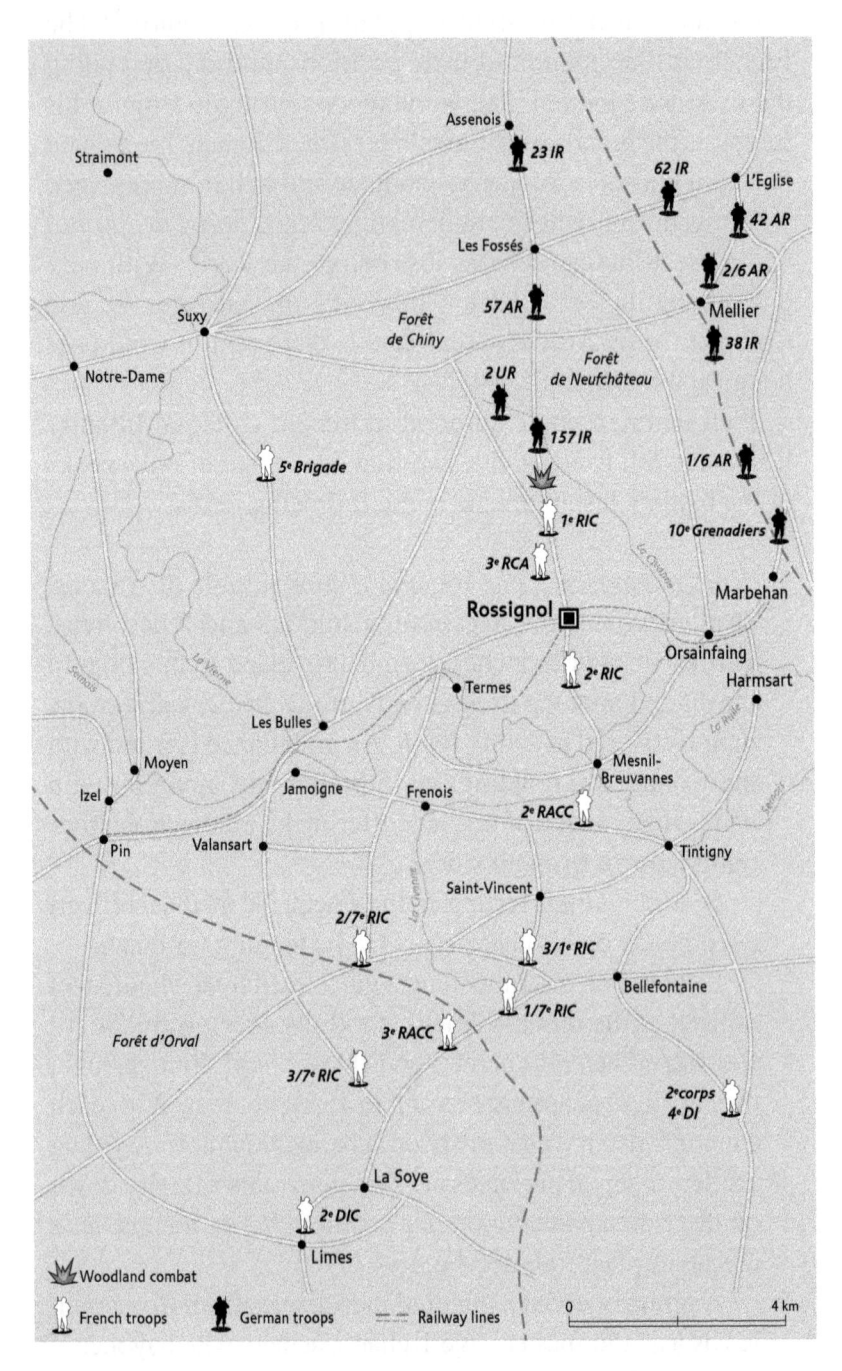

2 P.M.: Encirclement of the French troops at Rossignol

Breuvanne, and the gun fires its last shell. I make my way to a small thicket opposite the Germans and let myself go limp, dropping in a single movement, face first. The first German line reaches me and stops... I clench my teeth waiting for the finishing stroke, but they set off again.[32]

The German 11th and 12th Infantry Divisions now have Rossignol completely surrounded. The first groups of beleaguered soldiers begin to surrender. As a final act of desperation, they busy themselves with saving the regimental insignia from the ignominy of capture. The flag of the 1st Colonial Infantry Regiment is taken down. A sergeant wraps the silk around his torso under his greatcoat, while the medals are collected by an officer, Captain Charles Paris de Bollardière. As for the flag of the 2nd Colonial Infantry Regiment, it is simply buried, and will be recovered after the war.

Small groups of soldiers fall back to the river and cross the Semois by their own means, more or less covered by what remains of the divisional artillery at the outskirts of Saint-Vincent, itself protected by the 7th Colonial Infantry Regiment, which retreats at around 5.30 p.m. At around 7 p.m., the German troops, themselves also exhausted and having suffered heavy losses since going on the offensive, do not go after the French units. They set up their tents around Rossignol.

Bugle calls are heard. The Battle of Rossignol has ended.

Post-mortem

For a whole set of reasons, it is difficult to arrive at a precise figure for the French losses on 22 August during battle in the vicinity of Rossignol. Immediately afterwards, the battlefield was left in the hands of the Germans, who were more interested in gathering up their own dead than in counting French corpses. In addition, a portion of the injured would succumb to their wounds in the course of the following days, in both French and

German military hospitals; furthermore, given the inadequate nature of medical services at this time, few of them would manage to remain alive until they arrived at these facilities. The ratio of wounded to killed, which was about three or four to one for the entire duration of the war, was certainly a good deal lower that day. Especially since it seems that the Germans had actually finished off a certain number of the wounded on the battlefield.[33]

Apart from those taken prisoner, there is another large category, that of the 'missing in action'. Given the disorganization of the overall battle, this group may include men killed in action whose bodies would never be found, but also surviving soldiers like Corporal Failin who, left for dead on the battlefield, would evade capture by the Germans for nearly six months, with the assistance of local Belgian people. He is far from the only one to have had this kind of experience.

Consequently, French statistics tend to group all those not at roll call in their respective units the next morning in a vast category of 'killed, wounded, taken prisoner or missing in action', with the understanding that many of those taken prisoner were already wounded as well. In a book published in 1932, Alphonse Louis Grasset, who held the rank of colonel during the war, reports total losses amounting to 12,000 men for the Colonial Corps, of the 20,000 committed to the battle, including 11,500 for the 3rd Colonial Infantry Division alone (the remainder coming from the two regiments of the 2nd Colonial Infantry Division, which had continued to provide cover for most of the day, but who ran up against the advancing German forces towards dusk, sustaining heavy losses).[34] The Colonial Corps monument, erected to the north of Rossignol in 1927, refers to 6,473 dead for the 3rd Colonial Division, to which must be added a large majority of the 2,379 'missing in action', resulting in a probable total of about 7,000 killed that day for this division alone. To this figure must be added the 4,000 taken prisoner by the Germans.

The official French military analysis of the disaster has itself been adjusted in the years since the war. In the immediate post-war years, a consensus prevailed according to which the French, here as elsewhere in the Belgian Ardennes, had rushed headlong into long-established German defensive lines, and that once they had committed to the battle, the impulsive temperament of the French troops had led them to exhaust themselves in heroic, yet foolhardy, bayonet charges. It is this interpretation that colours the speech given on 9 September 1921 by Louis Laurens, who seven years earlier had served as a captain on General Raffenel's staff. Here is his description of the action in the forest of Neufchâteau (he did not personally take part in this fighting, as he found himself at his general's side, several kilometres behind the front line):

> Upon leaving Saint-Vincent, our dragoons had been steadily driving back the small groups of enemy cavalrymen dispatched from the squadron occupying Rossignol. This squadron rapidly fell back, chased by our men, who rushed into the forest behind them. All of a sudden a fusillade broke out, causing our dragoons to dismount and return fire with their carbines. Soon thereafter, they were joined by the entire advance-guard infantry. The battle then took on a violent character, unprecedented in its scale. From 7.30 a.m. to noon, the three battalions of the first regiment and two battalions of the second regiment, the latter having rushed to the aid of their fellow soldiers at around 9 a.m., confronted forces outnumbering them by more than two to one. The three battalion commanders and a large number of officers were killed at the outset. But our men, mowed down by a barrage of machine-gun fire coming from snipers cleverly hidden in the bushes, were not content to hold their positions. Raising the ante, they wanted at all cost to throttle the offensive of the invisible adversary taking such a heavy toll. Our men charged madly and heroically with bayonets, again and

again, hindered each time by the formidable firepower of the enemy, leaving gaping holes in their ranks, but not causing them to show any signs of discouragement, not the slightest hint of weakness. Upon viewing the resulting carnage, the survivors' only driving force was a burning desire to avenge their brothers in arms. But, as time passed, this task eluded their grasp. Despite their fearless exploits, the moment came when the leavings of these battalions, reduced to clumps of leaderless soldiers, were compelled to fall back to the village. Their retreat was effected very, very slowly. The enemy forces were so awed by their strength and tenacity that they followed them cautiously and decided to emerge from the woods only at about 3 p.m.[35]

In 1929, Lieutenant Louis Garros essentially made this same argument in a presentation on the Battle of Rossignol given at the Cercle Militaire de Rouen. However, he laid blame for the catastrophe on an unexpected party, but one with the advantage of exonerating the French chain of command of any responsibility: the fog. It is worth quoting in full his analysis of the battle, directly inspired by Victor Hugo's account of the Battle of Waterloo in his novel *Les Misérables*:

If there hadn't been any fog on the morning of 22 August 1914, and if the French Fourth Army had started advancing two hours earlier, the fate of the world would have been very different. All that was needed to unleash a cataclysm lasting four and a half years, during which men would be inculcated in the art of trench, chemical and submarine warfare, occasioning a military build-up encompassing most of the world's peoples and engendering a conflict spreading to the entire planet, was a little mist and the marching orders given to our regiment at 5 a.m. to plunge all these nations into an abyss of military, economic and social problems, in which they are still mired.

In the absence of fog, with the troops setting off instead at 3 a.m., the French forces would have had the time to cross the wooded areas before encountering the enemy, the cavalry would have been able to reconnoitre and actually collect the necessary information. And the battle would have been won.

How many mistakes were made by the French command contributing to the losses incurred? Is this shipwreck the fault of the captain? We don't think so.

[Joffre's] battle plan was, for all those having viewed it in detail, a masterpiece. Drive straight to the centre of the German line, create a breach in the enemy, cut its forces in two, direct the right flank to Belgium and the left flank to Metz, create two separate segments, carry Neufchâteau, seize Marche, cut off communications at Aachen – all of this was in the battle plan for the French chief of staff, after which it would be clearer where things stood.[36]

In 1935, General de Langle de Cary, the Fourth Army commander, more critical of Joffre, who it must be remembered had exiled him to Limoges, offered his own soberer analysis of the reasons for the disaster:

From my side and that of Third Army (but especially from my side), we launched an offensive over extremely difficult terrain: the forest of the Ardennes, a genuine hellhole, crossed by the Semois, creating an obstacle in our path. The enemy had already been in the forest for several days and, aided by the cover it provided, had established a defensive line encountered by several of our army corps, especially XVII Corps. It was hardly favourable attack terrain for an army. It meant the risk of serious miscalculations despite the military value of the troops. At the very least, the forest should have been investigated first. But the general in charge was against sending any personnel other than the cavalry. He wanted to ensure a surprise attack, and I had to yield to his reasoning. But our troops were the ones dealt the surprise, discovering barbed wire[37] and cleverly hidden machine guns in the forest. This does not excuse the mistakes committed by our side. For example, XVII Corps was fully ensconced in the forest without taking the most basic of precautions. The Colonial Corps, whose excellent regiments were not yet fully accustomed to the needs of continental warfare, especially with German armies as their adversaries, headed into the fray with magnificent gusto and temerity. It was inadequately covered on its right flank by II Corps, which was late to arrive and had to march in a zigzag path to boot. Also, it did not take advantage of information that might have been provided by the local population, nor of the protection that might have been afforded by the assigned cavalry regiment. This is the source of the terrible surprise which, despite the heroic dedication of the officers and the courage of the troops, caused the loss of nearly two-thirds of the 3rd Colonial Division.[38]

These French analyses call for a certain number of observations. The German troops were almost equal in number to those of the French and had arrived at the site of the battle at the same time. Once their reconnaissance, which was far more effective than that of the French cavalry, had revealed the state of the enemy positions (at about 7 a.m.), the Germans needed only an hour to set up a defensive line in the forest of Neufchâteau, and perhaps two hours to install their artillery guns on high ground, to the east and west of Rossignol. Thus the true reason for the different outcomes experienced by the French and the Germans that day in Rossignol was not an inequality of forces or equipment, but instead the far superior organization of the German command compared to its French counterpart.

At the same time, the 'magnificent gusto and temerity' of the colonial troops deserves a closer analysis. Although it is beyond question that, at the end of the day, groups of French soldiers charged with bayonets at the ready, trying to break the grip of the surrounding forces, it is highly unlikely that any such charge took place in the morning in the forest of Neufchâteau as the limitations of the terrain would not have made it possible. More than these certainly heroic bayonet charges, it seems that the extent of losses on 22 August was due to the equally heroic immobility of troops exposed for hours to artillery shelling, gradually compounded by advances of German riflemen, laying down dense and effective fire. Whatever the reason for the absence of any retreat order (incompetence, intellectual rigidity or gradual dissipation of the will of the French command), the colonial soldiers paid a heavy price that day for their determination not to break formation under fire in the absence of an order to do so.

As for the Germans, who as we have said committed nearly the same number of men as the French to the battle, the cumulative total of wounded and killed would rise to about 2,500 men out of action, about a third of whom were killed (and, logically, with very few taken prisoner). We thus find 700 German tombs in the cemeteries around Rossignol, for about 800 to 1,000 dead in all.[39]

The ratio of French to German losses is certainly appalling. However, it is important to note that the figure for German losses (sustained mainly during the second half of the battle, when the German riflemen came closer to the French lines, exposing themselves to fire) seemed extraordinarily high to their command. This had two major consequences. The first was to delay the German continuation of battle by at least twenty-four hours, as the commanders had concluded that their troops would be too severely affected to throw themselves into an attack on the French forces the next morning. This unexpected respite allowed the latter to regroup and reorganize themselves at the Franco-Belgian border before starting to fall back to the Marne, thus avoiding being routed immediately. The second was to incite the Germans to massacre Belgian civilians (inhabitants of Rossignol and its environs), as reprisal for the resistance encountered during the final assault. Already in the late evening of 22 August, 108 local people were captured and accused of being *francs-tireurs* ('free shooters'), suspected to have fired on German troops.[40] Piled into cattle cars, they were deported towards Germany. On the morning of 26 August, at Arlon station in Luxembourg, they were pulled out of the cars and lined up in groups of ten alongside an embankment to be shot to death.[41]

CHAPTER 3

FROM FRANKFURT TO ROSSIGNOL

The course leading the Colonial Corps to embark on its fateful journey through the Belgian Ardennes on 22 August 1914 was in fact set in motion outside Frankfurt's Hotel zum Schwan on 10 May 1871, at the signing of the treaty putting an end to the Franco-Prussian War. Although the local populations had no say in the matter, Alsace and the north-eastern portion of Lorraine were ceded to Germany.[42] The Germans thus annexed the French *départements* of Bas-Rhin and Haut-Rhin in Alsace, with the exception of the territory of Belfort; the *arrondissements* of Sarreguemines and Metz and the eleven communes of the *arrondissement* of Briey in Moselle; the *arrondissements* of Sarrebourg and Château-Salins in Meurthe; and the cantons of Saales and Schirmeck in the Vosges.

Previously claiming the Rhine as its 'natural' eastern frontier, France thus saw its border with Germany moved westward to the foot of the Vosges mountains, relinquishing 1,447,000 hectares (about 3,575,600 acres) of land, 1,694 communes and 1,587,000 of its people. It also gave up 20 per cent of its mining and steel potential. The terminus of the Rhône–Rhine canal was also now in hostile hands, cutting the link with the northern branch of the Canal de l'Est. In addition, France had to pay a 'war indemnity' of 5 billion francs. The cumulative result was therefore a loss of land, population, industrial potential and financial resources.

From the signing of the Treaty of Frankfurt and until August 1914, the willingness of either side to cross swords once again rose and fell, in tune with the ebb and flow of nationalistic sentiments and the changing state of international relations. In France, there was a gradual shift in the political climate from one dominated by secular, republican left-wing patriots calling for revenge on Prussia to one characterized by a nationalistic right viewing blood, soil and Catholicism as the foundation of national identity. But the establishment of the Franco-Russian Alliance also dates from this period, as does the signing of the agreement by Britain and France later to be known as the Entente Cordiale. And yet, throughout the period, general staff officers and governments on either side of the Vosges never stopped analysing the eventual conditions and circumstances of a new conflict, seen by both France and Germany as, if not desirable or unavoidable, at least as continually within the realm of possibility. It was clear that any new clash of arms would be shaped by geographical, demographic and diplomatic factors. Efforts pursued by military men to adapt to the terrain of a new conflict, to the play of alliances and the difference in demographic resources between the two countries, would in turn guide both German and French strategic choices.

Geographical organization based on fortifications

The Treaty of Frankfurt deprived France of its natural line of defence against an invasion from the east. The left bank of the Rhine, the Vosges range and the fortified site of Metz were all lost. The 1871 borders thus gave Germany avenues to invade France from the north-east. Concerned by this new vulnerability, the French authorities established a National Defence Committee bringing together elected officials and military authorities, which responded to the loss of natural protection previously offered by the Rhine and the Vosges with a programme for the establishment or renovation of a series of fortifications as a man-made alternative. Under the direction of General Raymond Séré de Rivières, a military engineer and visionary builder, a large number of fortified structures were built or refurbished throughout the country, from the Pas-de-Calais to the Pyrenees. Between 1874 and 1885, a total of 166 fortresses and forty-three smaller works were either built or rebuilt, and 250 new artillery batteries were installed. In the north-eastern corner of the country, a double line of forts was erected between Verdun and Toul in the north, and between Épinal and Belfort in the south. The aim was to force a potential German invasion into a narrow corridor between Toul and Épinal (known as the Charmes Gap), by creating a defensive line favourable to French troops massed in this area.

Undertaken with enthusiasm despite the financial burden for the French treasury,[43] this effort did not of course escape notice in Germany, where it deeply influenced strategic thinking on the way in which an offensive could be conducted in France without necessarily having to lay siege to these fortress lines, which would conceivably be long and costly from both an economic and a human standpoint. However, in France, the effectiveness of the defensive line put in place by Séré de Rivières was gradually called into question, given rapid progress in construction technologies, steel-making and the chemistry of explosives. The first forts in the programme were built of brick masonry; soon thereafter, the development of more destructive high-intensity explosives cast doubt on the capacity of these forts to resist the new nitroguanidine-based projectiles. Full-scale testing carried out in 1875 inspired the replacement of traditional masonry structures by applying new construction techniques using concrete, and later reinforced concrete. At the same time, the artillery batteries, initially placed in the open air within the polygonal structure of the forts, needed to be buried in the ground and covered with steel domes.

Until the outbreak of the war, the development and maintenance of fortifications in France was a subject of fierce debate, fuelled by their high cost at a time when the army needed to replenish its equipment and refurbish its barracks to contend with the nearly 50 per cent rise in military manpower, which occurred as a result of the law enacted in 1913, extending the period of time for mandatory military service from two to three years. Furthermore, due to continued technological progress, it was becoming difficult to determine when the development of fortifications would be outstripped by advances made in explosives. Many among the French general staff were opposed in principle to any strategy based on fortifications, due to its defensive character. Doubt was also cast on the logic behind spending fortunes on building fortified structures that would quickly become obsolete. And the caustic memory of the 1870 defeat still remained very much in mind, with French forces holed up in the Metz fortress, powerless against the excellent mobility of the Prussian army. For all these reasons, less emphasis was placed by the French on equipping fortifications from the turn of the twentieth century.

Demographic imbalance between France and Germany

Already in 1870, the total population of the various German states within the Reich exceeded that of France. A major preoccupation for French military planners, this imbalance was particularly inconvenient at a time when progress in social control enabled the rapid mobilization, by conscription, of an entire age group, while advances made possible by industrialization equipped forces with modern and more effective weapons. In order to assess the military potential of either side, demographic factors are therefore very important. The crux of the matter was that in 1914, France had a population of 39 million, whereas that of Germany had reached 69 million. Moreover, due to its higher birth rate, the German age pyramid was more favourable, with a greater proportion of young men.[44] In 1914, France had a maximum mobilizable potential of 5,110,000 men between the ages of eighteen and forty-eight, while in Germany this age group numbered 10,200,000.

However, when war was declared in August 1914, France had slightly more men called up for service than Germany (910,000 versus 870,000). This paradox is due to the entry into effect, in 1913, of the so-called 'three-year law' in France, which extended the term of military service by an additional year, whereas the Germans had retained a two-year military service. In addition, conscription was much more rigorous (or less selective, depending on your point of view) in France. In practice, regardless of the physical condition, family background or social standing of Frenchmen in the requisite age group, none could evade the republican duty of paying the *impôt du sang*, their 'blood tax' to the state. In Germany, by contrast, numerous grounds for exemption applied: budgetary concerns, continuation of studies, physical criteria, not to mention the wish to avoid giving the culture of firearms sway among a worker class whose loyalty to the regime was still open to question.

In the France of 1914, young men between the ages of twenty and twenty-three had to be on active duty; then they joined the reserve until the age of thirty-four. In principle, reservists were called to rejoin their units for refresher training or in the event of general mobilization. Between the ages of thirty-four and forty-eight, French reservists could still be mobilized, but only as part of a separate military organization, the territorial army.

As a result of its more favourable demographic situation, the German military system was very different. In peacetime, it was mandatory for men to serve in the regular army after their twentieth birthday for a two-year period (or three years if serving in the cavalry or field artillery), after which they would serve in the reserves for five years, followed by a further five years in the first levy of the *Landwehr* and seven years in the second *Landwehr* levy. At the age of thirty-nine, these reservists were transferred to the *Landsturm*, where they served until they turned forty-five (without annual training periods) and all military obligations were completed. About 40 per cent of German conscripts were exempted from active military service. This meant that they would be required to serve in the Ersatz Reserve for a period of twelve years. These German reserve units, comprising relatively young men in good physical condition, were liable to be called up for active duty when needed, whereas France's territorial units included only older reservists, often in their late forties, a large number of whom were farmers and manual workers, understandably quite worn out at this age.

France and Germany had very different perceptions of the military potential of their reservists, and the strategic choices embraced by either side also differed considerably. General staff officers in France, with little faith in the physical and technical quality of their reserve units, concluded that their mobilization would take too much time. They were also wary of a mass conscript army. Bitter memories of the Paris Commune lingered, and those of the 1907 mutiny by the 17th Infantry Regiment were even more acutely felt. In contrast, the Germans would not shy from combining their reserves with their first-line units. This choice having taken them by surprise, the French general staff, who had failed to understand the Germans' use of reservists and their integration with first-line troops, tended to underestimate German manpower and military strength during the first weeks of the conflict.

Complete reshaping of European alliances

After the French defeat in the Franco-Prussian War, the balance of power in Europe was altered, something that had important consequences for alliances over the next three decades, forged in some cases to maintain good relations and in others to gain the necessary support in the event of another war. For Germany, the status of country-to-country alliances determined the number of frontiers on which it would have to wage battle and the number of divisions it would need to commit to each front. On the French side, the successive governments of the Third Republic actively sought alliances and the possibilities were not always encouraging. Relations with Britain had certainly been strengthened under the Second Empire (particularly in connection with the joint move by the British and French to come to the aid of the Turks, dispatching their forces to the Crimea to battle the Russians), but the British were still often considered to be hereditary enemies, practically on a par with the Germans. As for relations between the Russian autocracy and republican France, thorny by nature, they were hardly eased by the traditional French sympathy for the cause of Polish independence. Emperor Wilhelm II, who had taken the reins of German diplomacy after forcing Bismarck's resignation as chancellor on 20 March 1890, offered France an unexpected windfall by deciding not to renew the Reinsurance Treaty with Russia that same year, which had bound both nations to neutrality. France seized the opportunity presented to sign a military convention with Russia in 1892; by 1894, they were formally aligned. Apart from military ties, this agreement fostered the development of growing economic relations between the two countries. In addition, although in a less formal way, France managed to further cement its ties with Britain, out of concern for Germany's colonial ambitions and the aggressive development of its naval power. Edward VII's accession to the throne in 1901 created a climate conducive to the signing of the Entente Cordiale three years later. Already in the last years of the nineteenth century, Germany had become aware that any conflict with France would very likely lead to war on its eastern frontier with Russia, and, if not on land, certainly at sea with Britain.

Schlieffen and the evolution of German military strategy

Count Alfred von Schlieffen (1833–1913), chief of the German general staff from 1891 until 1906, developed the military doctrine by which Germany could defend itself simultaneously on two fronts against France and Russia. His predecessor, Helmuth von Moltke (1800–91), the mastermind of Prussia's successful Austrian campaign of 1866 and the war against France in 1870–71, seemed convinced at the end of his life that a new conflict between France and Germany was becoming unlikely. In his view, advances in weapons, combined with the growth of the European economies, would turn any subsequent conflict into a prolonged war, so devastating in both human and economic terms as to make it unthinkable.[45] Schlieffen, who had joined the general staff in 1884 as the head of its military history section, saw things differently. His initial studies of France's heavily fortified border with Germany had led him to conclude that a direct assault on these fortifications would be too costly in human lives for the German army. His idea, both simple and bold, was thus to circumvent these fortifications from the north, sweeping through Belgium and the Netherlands to carry out quickly a strategic envelopment of opponent forces in France.

However, Belgium had been officially declared an independent and neutral state at the Conference of London in

January 1831, confirmed by the Treaty of London of 19 April 1839, under which the five great European powers – Great Britain, France, Prussia, Austria and Russia – had pledged to guarantee this neutral status. In addition, a German prince, Louis of Saxe-Coburg-Gotha, had been crowned the first king of the Belgians, under the name Leopold I. The Schlieffen Plan nevertheless entailed the violation of Belgium's neutrality (as well as that of the Netherlands), a decision that was grounded in two fundamental assumptions.

The first was that France had been, and would remain, Germany's chief rival. Even though, ultimately, German colonial ambitions would inevitably run up against those of Britain, Germany would need, first and foremost, to assert its military supremacy in Continental Europe by weakening France's military capacity. When the time came to take on Britain, Germany could count on the strength of the ever larger fleet of battleships being built up since the turn of the century under the supervision of Admiral Alfred von Tirpitz. Nevertheless, Schlieffen realized that the *Kriegsmarine* would need years of training before it would have any hope of emerging triumphant from any battle with the Royal Navy.

The second assumption was that Russia would honour its alliance with France and that Germany would have to wage war simultaneously on two fronts. Spurred by Alexander II's liberal reforms, Russian society was undergoing a massive social and economic transformation. Neither the violent spate of urban terrorist acts nor the defeat in the Far East at the hands of the Japanese army, nor even the 1905 revolution, had thrown a wrench into the wheels of Russia's rapid economic growth. This expansion was in large part financed by a considerable influx of French capital, in the form of subscriptions to Russian loans by French investors. Thus, from the Darwinian perspective of Wilhelmine Germany, in order to ensure the survival of German culture, a clash with Russia, as with Britain, was seen as inevitable. However, it was thought wiser to attack Russia fairly quickly, before its fast track to modernization had run its course.

But Germany had to deal with France first. Due to its vast size and the still primitive condition of its infrastructure, Schlieffen concluded that, in the event of war, Russia would be slower to mobilize its army. On the other hand, he felt that the French, with their modern rail network, would be able to mobilize their forces very quickly. The Schlieffen Plan was therefore based on the idea that, for the first few weeks of a war on both fronts, Germany could overcome France by committing most of its troops to a massive and rapid campaign in the west. The triumphant troops would then be shipped east by rail.

The Schlieffen Plan required that the fortress line in Lorraine be circumvented by attacking from the north. Apart from the intrinsic difficulty of this task, time would not be on the side of the German army, ruling out the possibility of laying siege, since German forces could certainly be attacked by a fully mobilized Russian army on the Eastern Front after a short while. Taking the long way around, by sweeping across Belgium and the Netherlands from the north, offered the most favourable route for a quick land offensive. Passing into France from the south, an alternative enveloping manoeuvre that had also been considered, in this case violating Swiss neutrality, would require moving troops across more difficult terrain, thus slowing their advance.

As for the victory over the French, their forces needed to be annihilated so that German troops could quickly move against the Russian army. Germany would have to triumph in a single, but decisive, battle. From a tactical standpoint, the German army could not allow any of the French troops to get away, since they might fall back to the area south of the Loire, for example, if given the chance, thus prolonging the conflict. Strategically, the victory needed to be of such a magnitude that it would completely rule out, and for some time, any possibility of retaliation.

The quick and decisive nature of the German manoeuvre was thus fundamental. There were three key elements necessary for implementing this strategy. The first of these was the optimal use of Germany's modern and effective railway system, designed according to a grid architecture,[46] which would allow for the rapid mobilization of troops to sweep into Belgium, and then, once France had been defeated, their rapid transfer to the Eastern Front. Secondly, German troops had to move westward quickly enough to encircle the French forces before they were fully ready. As a consequence, any military, or civilian, opposition to Germany's advance through Belgium had to be crushed with conviction. The third and last element was that the right wing of the German forces needed to be strengthened. In the gigantic sweep from the north conceived by Schlieffen, the right wing (the army advancing the furthest to the west) had to be especially strong. It would form the powerful fist that would crush the French army, already encircled by the other German forces. Its role, in accordance with the prevailing military doctrine, was to deliver a blow of maximum violence at the point of confrontation with the enemy. Thus it was at the edge of the attacking line that most of the German troops would be concentrated, leaving only a thin curtain of forces to face French troops in Alsace and in Lorraine. Accordingly, under the Schlieffen Plan, the right wing marching north through Belgium was to be seven times stronger than the left wing that would contain French troops in Alsace.

In sum, the main objective of the Schlieffen Plan was to overwhelm, encircle rapidly and then definitively annihilate the French forces, which it was assumed would be massed behind their fortresses in Lorraine, anticipating an attack from the east.

In his writings, Schlieffen often refers to the envelopment tactic used by Hannibal in his victory over the Romans at the Battle of Cannae in 216 BC.[47] Without a doubt, his plan was bold yet risky, requiring a complex operation to move two million men over several hundred kilometres of terrain, within a very tight time frame. As Schlieffen's German critics at the time – of whom there were more than a few – were at pains to point out, his plan was susceptible to the slightest malfunction, particularly in the event of any delay of execution, due to logistical problems or unexpected resistance by the Belgian army. Given recent advances in weapons, some among the German general staff had doubts about the possibility of leading a large-scale offensive without suffering catastrophic losses. But despite these concerns, the plan met with favour among political and military decision-makers, who envisioned a decisive victory at the end of a very violent but very short war.

Schlieffen's successor, Helmuth Johannes Ludwig von Moltke (1848–1916), often referred to as 'Moltke the Younger' to distinguish him from his celebrated uncle, adopted most of his predecessor's plan, although not without making a number of major changes.[48] The first was Moltke's decision to respect Dutch neutrality, confining the invasion route to Luxembourg and Belgium. Moltke also noted the constantly improving relations between France and Britain, cemented by the Entente Cordiale: he was convinced that the German invasion of Belgium would very likely bring Britain into the conflict on the French side. Even if, in the absence of conscription, the British would need some time in order to put troops in the field in large numbers, Germany would be immediately exposed to a potential sea blockade by the Royal Navy. It was therefore important to leave the Netherlands out of the conflict, so that it could serve as a conduit for maritime trade from and to Germany in the event of such a blockade, thanks to neutral vessels, such as those under the flag of the United States. The counter-effect of this choice was that, between the Belgian Ardennes and the Dutch southern border, there was only a narrow corridor – about twenty kilometres wide – through which to draw the 600,000 men of the German First and Second Armies, whose main mission would be to encircle and then annihilate the French forces. And this corridor passed through Liège, with its twelve forts. Knocking out these forts and capturing Liège therefore quickly became the overriding imperative at the beginning of the war.

Another difference between the approaches of Schlieffen and Moltke was that the latter felt that Russia would be able to mobilize its troops more quickly. Despite its defeat in the Russo-Japanese War, the revolutionary unrest in 1905 and various political vicissitudes, Russia was experiencing a period of remarkable industrial and economic development, spurred by its abundant natural resources. In particular, the development of its railway system, combined with improvements in its administrative infrastructure, caused Moltke to fear that Russian forces would be able to make an incursion into East Prussia much more quickly than initially supposed. Moltke therefore included in his plans the possibility of rapidly dispatching some units, if necessary, to the Eastern Front.

Increasingly, Moltke became convinced that, at the outbreak of the war, the French would not remain massed behind their Lorraine fortress line but instead, overrun by the cult of the offensive celebrated in their military literature, would at the very least be leading incursions into Alsace, and perhaps Lorraine, from the very start of the conflict. Moltke thus decided to strengthen his units in Lorraine and northern Alsace, bringing the ratio between these and the right wing down to 1:3, from Schlieffen's 1:7.[49]

Evolution of French military strategy

French military strategists weighed the same factors analysed by their German counterparts: geography, demography, alliances and industrial development. However, the French analysis resulted in very different decisions.

Until 1898, when Plan XIV was adopted, France maintained a chiefly defensive military strategy, given its demographic imbalance with Germany. This plan anticipated that fighting would be concentrated along the border with Germany, possibly including a French offensive to recapture Alsace. Plan XV, adopted in March 1903, was also defensive in nature, but broke new ground by considering the rapid deployment of reserve units. General Victor Michel, named commander-in-chief of the French army in 1906, was tasked with preparing Plan XVI, which was completed in January 1911 and presented to the Supreme War Council on 19 July. This plan included radical changes. Taking note of the alliances with Britain and Russia, Michel rightly suspected that the Germans were planning to sweep through Belgium and that they would aim to bolster their numerical superiority by using their reserve units from the very beginning of any conflict. Michel therefore proposed the complete mobilization of all reservists and their integration with active units so as to place men along the entire border with Belgium and effectively defend this broad front.[50] He thus planned to concentrate a million men between Lille and Rethel, with the option of a pre-emptive strike in Belgium in the event of a German attack. But these innovative ideas were seen as difficult to put into action, requiring considerable time for preparation, and met with resistance from superior officers, who were reluctant to use reservists in the manner proposed. Furthermore, many raised the point that even the potential entry of French troops into Belgium might be enough to scuttle the Entente Cordiale. Plan XVI was therefore unanimously rejected by the council. On 28 July, ousted from the Supreme War Council, Michel was also replaced as commander-in-chief by the council's youngest member: General Joffre.[51]

The choice of Joseph Césaire Joffre (1852–1931) was not an obvious one. Born in the French Pyrenees town of Rivesaltes, he was one of eleven children of a cooper. A gifted student from an early age, Joffre studied civil and military engineering at the École Polytechnique in Paris, after which he was attached to the French army's corps of engineers. Before completing his studies, he had been posted at one of the siege batteries during the Franco-Prussian War and later helped to build the series of fortifications in accordance with Séré de Rivières's plans. He followed this assignment with a long career as a Colonial Corps officer, first in Indochina, then in Madagascar and equatorial Africa. Hardly a military theorist, he was known as an effective administrator and as a good fortifications specialist. In fact, the logical choice to succeed Michel would have been General Joseph Gallieni, whose peers admired his intellectual prowess. Like Joffre, Gallieni had made his reputation in the colonies, where he had been Joffre's superior officer. But Gallieni declined to accept the position, giving as his reason the fact that he would be retiring in two years and thus would lack sufficient time for the task at hand. Gallieni then recommended the most senior military commander having attained the highest grade, General Paul Marie Pau. However, there were two obstacles to this choice. Pau had made it known that he wanted to make his own senior military appointments (until then the purview of the president of the Republic, acting on proposals from the war minister), and he was a devout Catholic. The issue here was that relations between the Third Republic's civil authorities and its military hierarchy had always been difficult. Seen as incompetent leaders for their conduct during the Franco-Prussian War, the generals, assumed to be monarchists and traditionalist Catholics, were also considered to be unconvinced of the effectiveness of the republican form of government. President Patrice de MacMahon's forced resignation in 1879 after his anti-republican attempts to rule against the National Assembly, war minister Georges Boulanger's departure into exile in 1889 after his plans for a putsch were revealed, the Dreyfus affair, to be sure, and the riots following the legal separation of church and state in 1905 had created a constant climate of suspicion surrounding the highest-ranking military leaders. In 1904, General Louis André, war minister in the government of Émile Combes, had been accused of compiling dossiers on church attendance by all garrison officers in France, with the assistance of the Masonic Grand Orient de France. The purpose of these dossiers was to favour the promotion of officers without anti-republican tendencies. In actual fact, it seems the dossiers did not play a determining role in these officers' careers. Quite a few openly Catholic generals were serving in important positions at the start of the war. This was notably the case for Ferdinand Foch, Édouard-Noël de Castelnau, whose ardent Catholicism had earned him the nickname 'le Capucin Botté' (the fighting friar), and Charles Lanrezac, whose virulent anti-Semitism had shocked his contemporaries, so outspoken was he, even by the standards of France during the Dreyfus affair. All these men were promoted without obstacle. But to the highest position in the military hierarchy, war minister Adolphe Messimy, a Saint-Cyr graduate who had become a Radical Socialist deputy, wanted to appoint someone the government could depend on. Joffre's republican credentials were considered unassailable and it was thought that he might also be a Freemason. He also maintained good relations with many of his more conservative peers. Joffre would thus be chosen as the new chief of the general staff.

Joffre and the 'all-out offensive'

Corpulent, phlegmatic in appearance, but capable of exploding into violent fits of temper when provoked, General Joffre's service record was not outstanding. But he would later demonstrate his talent for political manipulation, also proving himself an effective administrator. His mastery in this area allowed him to impose his strategy and his organizational choices. In the run-up to the war, he thus managed to assume complete control over the conduct of all operations. Due to his quasi-independence from political control as well as his absolute authority over his direct subordinates (the army commanders), Joffre enjoyed greater powers than those of Moltke, his German counterpart, whose generals were granted far more latitude and room for initiative than were officers holding the same positions in France (who had none of either). Furthermore, the authority of France's war minister had effectively been undermined by the government's continuing instability. Messimy, the war minister who had named Joffre in late July 1911, was reappointed in August 1914, thus becoming the fifth appointee to that role just since the beginning of that year. Within army ranks, Joffre was able to rely on the unwavering support of the youngest general staff officers, less affected by political concerns than their elders, but united by their shared adherence to the precepts of the 'all-out offensive'. This term refers to a tactical and strategic doctrine that had its roots as much in the cultural changes reshaping the country as in advances in weapons technology.

In 1906, Colonel Loyzeau de Grandmaison, who headed the war ministry's operations branch, which saw to the preparation of border defences as well as the French army's annual manoeuvres (simulated combat between units), published a book entitled *Le dressage de l'infanterie en vue du combat offensive* (The training of the infantry for offensive combat), which he later used and expanded upon in two conferences for staff officers in 1911 at the Centre des Hautes Études Militaires (CHEM).[52] These two conferences, written up and published that same year, were enthusiastically received in military circles. Colonel (later Marshal) Foch, who held the title of chief instructor (1896–1901) and then commandant

(1908–11) at the École Supérieure de Guerre, was also a leading exponent of this same concept, profoundly influencing an entire generation of officers who would soon be called up to command units destined to take part in the war.

As was also true for the Germans, the lethal capacity of weapons was a major preoccupation for military planners. Was a modern war still possible without exhausting the demographic and economic resources of the belligerents? Like the Germans, the French concluded in the affirmative, provided that the war was quick, violent and decisive. But where the Germans placed the emphasis on the excellence of a quick and brutal attack, French strategists were more focused on a state of mind. Hence their preference, when engaging the enemy, for an immediate and frontal attack, led by the infantry, without necessarily taking the time to prepare the artillery batteries, as this might slow down operations.

Various historical, anthropological or philosophical considerations also entered into the development of strategy on the French side. The theorists of the all-out offensive had been inspired by the successes of the Revolutionary and Napoleonic armies. At a time when social-Darwinist race theory held sway, it was tempting to assume that there was a typically French way of war, harking back to the *furia francese* forged on battlefields in Italy during the Renaissance. In short, French soldiers saw themselves as destined to topple triumphantly enemy troops both greater in number and better equipped (all the more so since, historically, these had often been Germanic tribes) through a frontal and recklessly courageous attack. *Études sur le combat*, an influential and innovative critique of prevailing French military theory on the basis of detailed information about actual conditions in the battlefield, was published posthumously in 1880 (and reissued in several editions until the outbreak of the war).[53] Its author, Charles Ardant du Picq, a French colonel and military analyst with a particularly subtle understanding of the behaviour of men in battle, who was himself killed in an engagement near the beginning of the Franco-Prussian War, noted that the side with the superior 'resolution to advance' would always triumph. No longer alive to comment upon the finer points of his analysis, Ardant du Picq's concepts were freely adapted and used by young military theorists to claim the inherent superiority of troops consisting of individuals maintaining an offensive stance at all times. During the same period, the philosopher Henri Bergson's reputation had reached a high point, his concept of an élan vital, or life force, fascinating those who hoped that this form of energy would always allow man to dominate the material world, and by extension the battlefield, that characteristically French superhuman courage would triumph over German materiel superiority. However, against the backdrop of this vaguely neo-Romantic intellectual climate, some partisans of the all-out offensive based their strategic conclusions on a more materialistic analysis. They noted that France, at a demographic disadvantage and less advanced industrially than Germany, did not have the resources for a war of attrition. The decision to favour an offensive stance was therefore also a logical (albeit questionable) conclusion reached on the basis of clear-minded demographic and economic observation. Some superior officers were even plainly opposed to this primacy of morale over manoeuvre, including Philippe Pétain, then a colonel, and General Lanrezac, the latter noting curtly that 'if every corps commander has the right and the duty to rush the first enemy he meets, it is difficult to imagine how the commander-in-chief could direct operations given this approach'.

The concept of the all-out offensive had a strong influence on the shape of the French military's newest war plan, known as Plan XVII. Its impact was also felt on the development of artillery regiments: on their discipline, their mode of command and the choice of equipment. Despite the popular notion to the contrary, the French entered into the war with a complement of artillery as strong as that of the Germans, but its composition was different, because it was focused on offensive support. Its main component, the quick-firing 75-mm field gun, effective at short distances and very mobile, was thus the ideal weapon to accompany infantry assaults. Conversely, the lack of long-range artillery and the low number of howitzers able to reach the opposite side of a ridge severely penalized the French in the war of positions. Furthermore, the cult of the offensive implied a rigid command hierarchy and unconditional obedience by the men. In the title of his book, Grandmaison's choice of the term *dressage*, normally used to refer to breaking in animals or disciplining children, speaks volumes. Subordinates must not ask any questions, nor trouble themselves with taking initiatives, but instead enthusiastically follow the order to attack when it is given.[54] French strategists were nonetheless aware that, on the modern battlefield, the 'fog of war' made it difficult to see and hear: they knew that the density of firepower required that attack formations be dispersed widely. Until the end of the Napoleonic era, attack formations consisting of compact lines allowed officers to advance, all the while keeping their men to hand. The more scattered formations of the modern era (lines of riflemen) left many soldiers out of sight – and thus out of voice range – of their officers. The latter thus needed to be that much more visible, moving out in front of their men and commanding by example. As for the soldiers, they could only follow blindly. This concept of the all-out offensive also helps to explain why the French entered the war in 1914 dressed in red peaked caps, blue coats and bright-red trousers. For some years already, the Germans had abandoned their traditional uniform colours in favour of *feldgrau* (field grey), while the British had replaced their bright-red tunics with khaki, brought back from India. The first reason for French conservatism in this regard was, as is often the case, financial. At a time when the law extending the term of mandatory military service from two years to three weighed heavily on the budget for the French army, which thus had to house and equip half again as many active soldiers, it was difficult to renew the entire stock of uniforms. Besides, traditionalists objected to dispensing with the colourful uniforms, which were thought to instil soldiers with enthusiasm and the civilian population with pride. But theorists of the cult of the offensive were also reticent to dress infantrymen in uniforms enabling them to better avoid the gaze of their superior officers or their enemies, in short to be tempted to conceal themselves in the face of fire and adopt a defensive stance.

Lastly, French military doctrine was influenced by the careful study of the twentieth century's first conflicts, and in particular the land battles of the Russo-Japanese War in 1904–5. Both sides suffered heavy casualties in this war, which opposed two armies undergoing rapid modernization: the Russians with the assistance of the French, and the Japanese with the help of the Germans. The two belligerents allowed observers from major powers not taking part in the conflict to monitor the hostilities, as was already the case for annual training manoeuvres. France thus dispatched a military mission, its members sent to different battle sites, tasked with analysing the impact of modern weapons, which were being used on a large scale for the first time. The observations of these envoys resulted in a series of detailed reports, grouped under the heading *Enseignements de la guerre russo-japonaise* (Lessons of the Russo-Japanese War).[55] Analysed by Olivier Cosson, these reports bring into relief very clearly the impact of military modernization (particularly the massive use of machine guns), and its consequences for the outfitting of soldiers and their living conditions.[56] However, the judgement of the reports' authors, although very lucid from a technical standpoint, is coloured for tactical matters by a Eurocentrism overlaid with narrow-minded prejudice. For the French observers, the Russian and Japanese armies were certainly adequately equipped and trained, but the soldiers on the field, on either side, were still Asians and thus unable, as noted by General Lombard, the commander of the military mission, to 'create a Napoleonic event'. Although the mission was able to arrive at a precise assessment of the effectiveness of field artillery and machine guns, its findings were deemed nevertheless inapplicable to French forces. This is strikingly demonstrated by the following conclusion, penned by General Lombard:

> Based on my observation of battles in this war, I have come to the conclusion that the characteristics of modern combat are eminently well suited to the temperament of our soldiers [...] I am also convinced that our infantrymen have an offensive capacity greater than that of their Japanese counterparts, remarkable though they may be. Among the latter, one does not find anything like our *furia francese*, the bravura stance that leads us to accomplish prodigiously bold exploits and spread terror among our adversaries. Without a doubt, even granted this fury, our military actions today need to be prepared with extreme care and prudence. Any failing in an attack of this type would be punished by the destruction of the assailing force. But if the attack is well managed I think that, given the qualities of our race, it could not help but prevail.[57]

Put simply, for General Lombard, recent developments in firepower did cast doubt on a tactical plan inspired by the cult of the offensive... unless it was to be executed by French soldiers.

Plan XVII

On 18 April 1913, it was Joffre's turn to present the first draft of his own war plan, which would be known as Plan XVII, to the Supreme War Council. His proposal was ratified by the council on 2 May. However, due to its complexity, especially from a logistical standpoint, making the many elements of his plan difficult to implement, the final version would only be completed on 1 May 1914.[58]

Plan XVII, in contrast to the Schlieffen Plan, was not an operational plan. It did not aim to lay out an entire campaign in accordance with a detailed chronology culminating in the defeat of the enemy and the final victory. It is best viewed as a concentration plan, establishing the composition of the various forces, their initial deployment positions and the means by which they would be assembled on the front.[59] The plan clearly indicates the French army's intention to carry out an offensive strategy, without entering into greater detail. The document phrases the main objective as follows: 'Whatever the circumstances, it is the commander-in-chief's intention to advance with all available forces united to attack the German armies.' The plan thus did not commit Joffre to any particular course of action, allowing events to determine how he would deploy his forces. Keen to give himself maximum discretion, Joffre took care to ensure that his decisions would not be set in stone by pre-established plans, and less still by his subordinates. For as long as possible, he would leave not only them but the war ministry itself in the dark as to his intentions.

Plan XVII grouped the north-eastern French forces into five armies. From right to left, it placed the French First, Second, Third and Fifth Armies along the German, Luxembourg and Belgian borders. The Fourth Army was to remain in reserve between the Second and Third Armies, from where it could move to the left if the Germans came through Belgium or to the right if, as some feared, they decided to invade Switzerland. Two groups, each consisting of three reserve divisions (territorial units) were to be placed on either side of the line. Finally, a group of three cavalry divisions was to be assembled to the left of the Fifth Army, in order to be able to move rapidly against German forces if they came through Belgium. In addition to these five armies, the French commander-in-chief could count on the support of four additional armies, which would take a bit of time to deploy. Three of them were stationed in North Africa. The fourth was positioned in south-eastern France, opposite the Italian border. If Italy decided to renege on its commitments to its German and Austro-Hungarian partners in the Triple Alliance, these troops would be immediately transported to north-eastern France.

Lastly, a secret annex to Plan XVII set out the details of the eventual participation of British forces (*'l'armée W'*) alongside their French counterparts. But this was hardly guaranteed. The 1904 Entente Cordiale did not ensure the same level of commitment between its two parties as did the Franco-Russian Alliance. It was especially concerned with settling colonial conflicts outside Europe.

The commitment by the British to military involvement on the Continent was far from certain. Until the outbreak of the war, it remained subject to the deliberate violation of Belgium's neutrality by the Germans. And until at least 1911 it continued to be contested by the Royal Navy, which favoured a strategy of purely naval confrontation with Germany, thus one that would be under its direction. That strategy was founded upon a naval blockade accompanied by raids on the main German ports, with the possibility of putting land forces ashore, if necessary. The matter was decided by prime minister Herbert Asquith on 23 August 1911, in opposition to the navy's preferred strategy, at a special meeting of the Committee of Imperial Defence, which resulted in the ousting of the First Lord of the Admiralty. French and British military leaders thereafter met on several occasions to discuss the strength and deployment conditions for an expeditionary force to France. Great Britain was the only major European power still relying on a small professional army (six infantry divisions) dedicated to the defence of the colonies (and potentially their

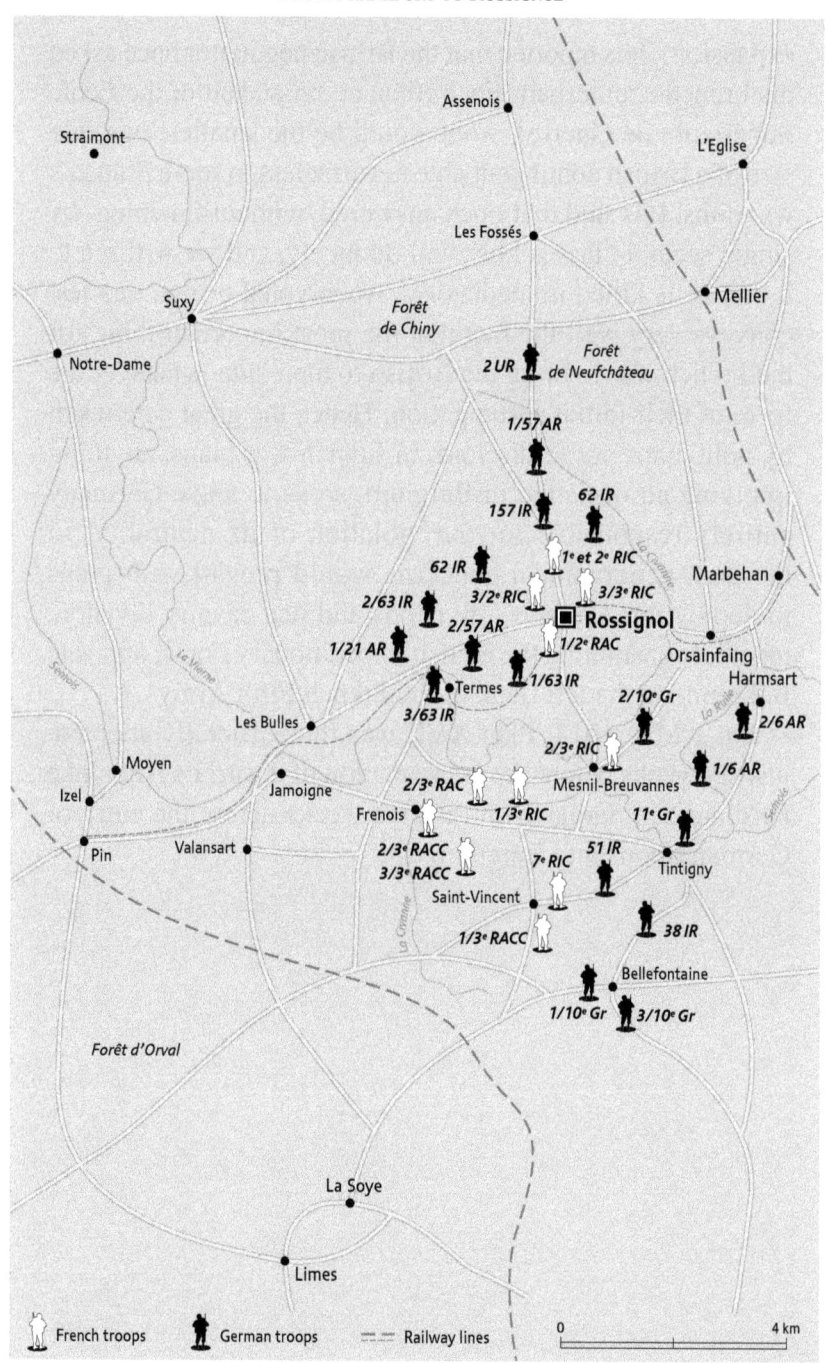

THE INITIAL OFFENSIVE PLANS OF THE FRENCH AND THE GERMANS BEFORE THE FIRST WORLD WAR

expansion). It is reported that the British negotiator once asked his French counterpart, Foch (then commandant of the École Supérieure de Guerre), what would be the smallest possible size of a British contingent able nevertheless to serve France's war aims. It is said that Foch answered, without flinching, 'A single second-class soldier will do nicely, and we will see to it that he is killed immediately.' Apocryphal or not, this jest conveys very well the fact that the most important thing for the French was to bring the British to their side, whatever the form of their initial participation. Hence the great care taken by politicians not to disclose, in French war plans, anything implying an initiative in Belgium, so as to leave Germany entirely responsible for the violation of its neutrality. In the end, geographical concerns would prevail with plans to deploy three infantry divisions and one cavalry division, together constituting the British Expeditionary Force, opposite Belgium, on the left flank of the French Fifth Army.

On 1 May 1914, Plan XVII was thus officially adopted, just six weeks before the assassination of Austria's Archduke Ferdinand in Sarajevo and twelve weeks before the entry of German troops into Belgium.

CHAPTER 4

WEAPONS AND ORGANIZATION

In order to analyse the day's fighting on 22 August, it is important first to gain an understanding of how the French and the Germans were armed and organized for war. Military equipment and organization had seen considerable changes in the previous century, but the weapons in use in 1914 by the two adversaries were relatively similar. Furthermore, the complement of equipment available to each army was nearly equivalent. However, there were significant contrasts in the doctrines applied for the deployment of these weapons and their use. The organization of French and German armies, the ways in which they moved and deployed their forces, and their command approaches reveal differences with serious consequences for the encounters on 22 August.

Rifles

As the key infantry weapon handled by individual soldiers, the rifle passed through several important stages in its development over the course of the nineteenth century. The Revolutionary and Napoleonic wars had been waged, on the French side, by troops equipped with the Charleville 1777 musket designed, as was a new range of artillery introduced at the same time, by the engineer Jean-Baptiste de Gribeauval. French soldiers at Waterloo were thus equipped with muskets about 150 centimetres long able to shoot large-calibre (17 mm) lead balls using a charge of black powder with an optimal range of 150 metres and a maximum range of 250 metres. In order to be effective, muskets needed to be presented and fired simultaneously by ranks of soldiers either standing or kneeling. A troop well trained in the handling, loading and reloading of these weapons could fire once every twenty to thirty seconds, thus between two and three rounds per minute. Attackers advancing on foot could cover between fifty and 100 metres between rounds.

Beginning in the 1890s, small-calibre (8 mm or less) repeating rifles, with bolt-action mechanisms and equipped with spring-loaded magazines, came into widespread use in Europe. The Lebel rifle, adopted by the French army in 1886 and updated in 1893, could fire up to twelve rounds a minute. Even more modern, the German Mauser (1898 model) and the British Lee–Enfield, in the hands of a well-trained soldier, could fire as many as fifteen rounds a minute. With the development of modern, more powerful and smokeless powders, the effective range of rifles increased considerably. By 1914, it had reached between 600 and 1,400 metres.[60]

To a large extent, the effective range of a rifle, and its rate of fire, varied depending on the level of training completed by the foot soldier. In this area, there were very significant differences from one country to the next in 1914. At the start of the war, British soldiers were professionals schooled in the importance of accurate and rapid rifle fire, a primordial aspect of their training.[61] On several occasions in Belgium, at Le Cateau and on the outskirts of Antwerp for example, the soldiers of the British Expeditionary Force inflicted heavy casualties on German troops owing to the effectiveness of their musket fire. As a matter of principle, the Imperial German Army was reluctant to train a large number of its recruits in the effective use of rifles, since a growing proportion of these men were from working-class backgrounds and their loyalty to the Wilhelmine Reich was far from certain. Nevertheless, over the twenty years preceding the war, Germany developed an extensive programme of drill exercises, for both active and reserve units, with strong emphasis on rifle training. On the French side, from a materiel as well as an ideological standpoint, training was focused instead on the handling and use of bayonets. This approach was in keeping with the military doctrine of the *offensive à outrance* (all-out offensive), which favoured forward motion and hand-to-hand combat. Sheer dash, courage and nerve were considered sufficient to defeat the enemy. This also meant that not too much money would be spent by the French on weapons for training periods, against the backdrop of serious budget constraints in the early 1900s. These differences in military doctrine led to contrasts in the way the nations involved approached the technological development of individual weapons. For the French, a rifle, even a modern one, was above all something that could be fitted with a bayonet and handled by a fiercely determined soldier. For the Germans, the concept of the concentration of firepower was paramount, bringing the combined force of individual weapons, machine guns and field artillery to bear against the same adversary.

MACHINE GUNS

While rifles evolved considerably in the nineteenth century, the appearance of machine guns in the last quarter of the century was nothing short of revolutionary. As noted by Stéphane Audoin-Rouzeau, with a rate of fire between 400 and 600 rounds per minute, not even the most accurate and disciplined combination of individual rifle fire could hope to hold its own against the effectiveness of such a weapon.[62] From the 1880s, the introduction of the American Maxim, a modern version of which would be used by the Germans, the British Vickers and the French Hotchkiss and Saint-Étienne marked the arrival on battlefields of weapons able to halt the advance of enemy troops completely. However, machine guns did present a number of major disadvantages, the first being weight – not only that of the gun itself, which was considerable, but that of all the elements required when the machine gun was put to use: its mounting tripod, the protective steel shield for the gun crew, belts and other accessories including spare barrels, together with a huge quantity of cartridges. As a result, machine guns were not especially mobile, particularly those available at the start of the war. Since it was difficult to move these weapons quickly, machine guns would be used mainly for defensive purposes and were not well suited to accompanying attacks by advancing troops. In addition, the machine gun's complex rapid-firing mechanism was very fragile. It jammed easily and broke down fairly often. The barrel tended to heat up quite rapidly and often needed to be replaced. Lastly, personnel operating machine guns were particularly exposed, since in battle most of the enemy's firepower would be focused on these weapons. In spite of this, there was never a shortage of volunteers to man this very exposed position.[63]

Field Artillery

Stéphane Audoin-Rouzeau has given us an authoritative analysis of the impact on the conduct of the entire war of exploding artillery shells: 'balls of steel blasted into the air, lighting up the sky, with a unique rumbling sound generated by the high speed at which they travelled'.[64]

Even more so than individual weapons, field artillery

underwent fundamental changes following the end of the Napoleonic Wars. Advances in science (especially in chemistry), combined with industrial developments (particularly of iron and steel metallurgy), brought about profound transformations in the characteristics of artillery and the way in which it was used. These developments addressed every, or nearly every, aspect of this weapon. The first focus was on the nature of the projectile, with solid cannonballs being replaced by hollow artillery shells. Powders were the next area of attention, with the introduction of explosives made from the mixture known as melinite in the 1880s. These explosives were far more powerful than those used previously and emitted much less smoke. At the end of the nineteenth century, a new problem emerged for the conduct of battle: the need to determine the location of the enemy's artillery batteries in order to launch a counter-attack. The effective range of artillery increased considerably. Accuracy was also improved, as advanced manufacturing techniques were able to produce better barrels with grooved interior walls, complemented by modern sighting equipment. Until that time, in order to absorb at least some portion of the weapon's recoil, the carriage needed to be very heavy, using significant quantities of metal, making the piece difficult to move and to install in the battery. The emergence of recoil-absorption systems involving hydraulic cylinders helped with this aspect and also allowed the gun to stay on target, avoiding the need to adjust and relay the piece after the recoil of each shot.[65] Thus the rate of fire increased considerably and, with it, the weapon's destructive capacity.[66] These developments also meant that pieces could be lighter in weight and therefore more mobile, in principle, to accompany attacking infantry. However, this development would also lead to a nearly exponential rise in the consumption of ammunition.

In 1914, the German army had 7,700 pieces of artillery at the ready, while France had 4,300. By 1918, these figures would be 20,000 and 14,000, respectively. But the artillery in the French arsenal was quite different from that of the Germans. French artillery mainly consisted of 75-mm guns, 3,800 of which were available in 1914. These were lightweight and relatively mobile pieces of artillery, offering a high rate of fire, able to quickly reach twenty rounds per minute, with an effective range as long as nine kilometres.[67] The 75-mm gun was an ideal weapon to accompany attacking infantry. But it was a weapon designed for direct firing at visible targets. The maximum elevation of its barrel was sixteen degrees, this rather flat trajectory preventing its rounds from hitting targets on the downward slopes of hills. On hilly and rough terrain, as in the Belgian Ardennes, batteries of these 75-mm guns had to get very near to the German lines in order to fire directly on them, thus exposing the gun crew to rifle fire from enemy infantrymen. The German army had a very similar piece, the Krupp 77-mm gun, with just slightly lower specifications in terms of its effective range and rate of fire. But the German army was also equipped with larger artillery. According to German military strategy, these heavier pieces served two purposes. The first of these, mainly met by 150-mm howitzers, which gave shells curved trajectories, was to fill the need for a siege weapon and to breach fortifications. This type of artillery played a decisive role at the beginning of the war, allowing the German army to pulverize the fortresses protecting Liège, followed by those around Namur and Maubeuge. Their shells were particularly effective: designed to be fired at short range, their metal casings could be relatively lightweight and thus contain a very high proportion of explosives.[68] The second, more defensive, purpose was fulfilled by long-range artillery, used to defend fortified positions and also for hitting targets on the downward slopes of hills. The French army, entirely offensive in posture, had no intention of leading a siege war against the Germans, and thus had not planned for artillery that might be used for such a purpose. In 1914, the French army only had about a hundred 155-mm pieces (the Rimailho 1904 model) and about two hundred 120-mm pieces. However, the French fortified sites of Nancy, Toul and Verdun had traditionally been equipped with large-calibre guns. But the French commanders were sceptical as to the usefulness of these fortified sites, and thus the artillery equipping them. On the one hand, continuing advances in explosives led the commanders to conclude that, in any event, these forts built around 1880–90 would not be able to withstand the more recently introduced explosives. On the other hand, the 1870 defeat was interpreted as resulting from the abandonment of strategic initiative by French generals at the time, Marshal Bazaine having allowed himself to be trapped with his men in the besieged fortress of Metz. Adamant about maintaining an offensive stance, the general staff was little concerned with the maintenance and modernization of artillery equipping these fortresses. However, the naval guns installed at Nancy would prove to be quite useful, in late August 1914, in helping Castelnau's Second Army, ably covered by Foch's XX Corps, repel the German forces attempting to capture the site and thus retain control of the Grand Couronné.

But from the beginning of the war, rather than the specific model of artillery used, it was the shells fired, and more precisely their availability in industrial quantities, that were the decisive factor. Fifty thousand shells were fired each day by French artillery in September 1914. In 1918, the average daily consumption had reached 190,000 shells. During the final German offensives, this figure would rise to 220,000 shells per day. Under these conditions, the continuation of the war required a munitions industry running at full capacity. In all, more than 330 million shells would be fired by French artillery over the course of the war.[69] Taking into account German, British and American artillery, nearly a billion shells landed on French territory during this period.[70] These developments would make the cannon the First World War's iconic weapon. More precisely, these exploded shells would be responsible for more than two-thirds of the war's casualties.

However, mobility was one area in which improvements had not been made – far from it. For one thing, artillery was still mainly drawn by horses. For another, the weight of artillery pieces tended to increase in line with their destructive capacity and, with the rise in rates of fire, more ammunition needed to be immediately available. This equipment had to be transported by additional men and horses. The following description of a French artillery battery in August 1914, consisting of four 75-mm guns, is particularly illuminating:

It was a beautiful spectacle, like a parade. First came the officers, their underlings and the trumpeters on their regimental horses. These were followed by the first piece of artillery, consisting of a gun wagon with its ammunition wagon, flanked by the subaltern or non-commissioned officer with responsibility for this weapon. The carriage, the same one normally drawn by two horses, here used a six-horse hitch, driven from the seat of the limber or by a man mounted on the first horse on the left. The artillerymen – the drivers and the gun crew – were seated on the benches of the ammunition chests. Once this first piece had passed, it was succeeded by three others, followed by two wagons, which together formed the 'fifth piece', consisting of elements other than guns or supplies. The artillery battery thus consisted of these five pieces. Next came the echelon: six heavy wagons loaded with chests full of shells, each drawn by six strong horses, and then the forge and the store wagon conveying tools, spare parts and materials necessary for making repairs. As part of any regiment's procession of vehicles, the general service wagon and three provisions carriages took up the rear, conveying all commissary items needed to make and serve coffee, soup and stew.[71]

In the first days of the war, especially during the battles in the Ardennes, the wooded, hilly terrain, compounded by the surprise encounters with the enemy, highlighted the difficulties faced by French forces in getting their artillery into position quickly. The Germans, who used similar equipment, proved to be much more efficient at this task, and would often be the first to engage. Given the destructive capacity of modern weaponry, this difference would have catastrophic consequences for their adversaries. In the trenches, the inadequate mobility of artillery, even as motorized transport was gradually being introduced, combined with the destruction of battlefields, would prevent the French from taking advantage of the rare openings found here and there over time. Unable to move their artillery forward rapidly, none of the belligerents were successful at protecting their infantry beyond a distance of a few kilometres from their point of departure. To do so would require a mobile, motorized, fully tracked and armoured artillery: in other words, tanks, which would only begin to appear in the summer of 1918.

ORGANIZATION, TRANSPORT AND COMMAND OF TROOPS

At the start of the First World War, infantry divisions were the basic tactical elements used by the French army. On 2 August 1914, France had mobilized forty-five active, twenty-five reserve, eleven territorial, two colonial and ten cavalry divisions – a total of ninety-three divisions. Each division itself comprised four infantry regiments, each with three battalions, to which were added one field artillery regiment, one cavalry squadron and one unit of engineers. The strength of a single division was about 15,000 combatants, including 280 officers.

Each division also had about 3,500 horses, thirty-six field guns and more than 500 wagons. In short, a lot of men and equipment to transport. In 1914, armies advanced mainly in two ways. First on foot, for infantrymen, with very heavy loads of assorted equipment (up to forty kilograms) on their backs.[72] Next on horseback, for the cavalry and the artillery. Each of these two regiments, particularly the artillerymen, needed to haul a number of wagons for special purposes (ammunition, feed for the horses and so on). The various elements of crew equipment were also drawn by horses. In order to determine the pace at which these infantry troops would have been able to advance, Terence Zuber has analysed the rules for German infantry deployment, with the understanding that these data would be similar for the French infantry.[73] An infantry troop had to advance in four columns, at a speed, depending on the terrain, of ten to twelve minutes per kilometre, thus five to six kilometres per hour. The supply wagons would be expected to follow at a pace of about four kilometres per hour. In the days preceding 22 August, German and French troops converging towards each other covered as much as forty kilometres each day. This corresponds to eight effective hours of marching per day, under the heat of the August sun, carrying a pack weighing as much as forty kilograms, for men of typical stature and physical condition for the early twentieth century. In addition, more than half of these men were reservists, sometimes over forty years of age, called up less than three weeks before. Thus, on either side, the foot soldiers fighting each other on 22 August must have been in a state of extreme fatigue. Moreover, soldiers in 1914 advanced in long columns on narrow routes that had not been designed for vehicular traffic. They thus marched four abreast. Consequently, regiments were spread out, at any given moment, over about one and a half kilometres, and even as much as two kilometres, including the munitions wagon. The length of an advancing division whose advance-guard unit had distanced itself slightly from the rest of the troops would stretch over more than fifteen kilometres. But the battles in late August 1914 were very often the result of surprise encounters, opposing troops stunned to find themselves face-to-face with the enemy. Given that a division attacked over a front of two to three kilometres depending on the terrain, for an entire division to enter into battle formation would thus take nearly three hours. The side able to deploy its troops more quickly would enjoy an advantage that could turn out to be decisive. This would often be the case for the German troops.

In August 1914, the Germans enjoyed a triple advantage in terms of officering, training and command structure. With respect to the first category, one of the German army's strengths during both of the twentieth century's world wars lay in its corps of subalterns and non-commissioned officers, especially the *Feldwebels*, similar to company first sergeants in the US system. Germans in these ranks were present in large numbers, in an actual ratio of about two to one compared to the French army, whose units rarely achieved their theoretical quotas of active officers, subalterns and non-commissioned officers.

For some twenty years prior to the conflict, the officer's profession had been losing its attractiveness among the French population. Recruitment ran dry in part as a result of a combination of several factors: the upheavals touched off by the Dreyfus affair, the complex and flawed management of military careers by the civil authorities, budgeting problems and mediocre pay. Apart from being present in greater numbers than their French counterparts, German subalterns and non-commissioned officers were also particularly well trained. The German army, relying on the nation's demographic strength, left a significant portion of each age class in reserve units. Once this distinction had been made between men suited for active duty and those assigned to reserve formations, the training programmes and drill sessions intended to maintain the readiness of these reserve troops on a par with that of active forces were more intense and frequent than those in France. The French army had twenty-six drill grounds while the Germans had twenty-eight, but the German army's grounds were twice as large as those of the French, on average. The German capacity to carry out coordinated campaigns of manoeuvre involving both active and reserve units as well as artillery was therefore much greater, and frequently used. The subalterns heading up these campaigns were superbly trained. In recognition of their prowess, the German command relied greatly on them for the management of an engagement. On the German side, the transmission of orders included a general explanation of the scheme of manoeuvre. The understanding of the aim pursued allowed each subaltern to adapt the conduct of the campaign to facts on the ground without waiting for detailed orders from on high. In contrast, the French system of command was as hierarchical as the German system was decentralized. The French general staff managed the conduct of battle. Whereas the German doctrine of engagement focused on an enveloping movement, the French doctrine sought to break through the enemy's defensive lines. It relied in part on maintaining troops in reserve, whose mobilization would allow the full attack to be made when the time came. General staff officers, benefiting from a centralized perspective, were the ones to decide upon the place and time to use these reserves. The French command system was therefore naturally hierarchical. Instructions received from on high, thus from quite a distance during the war of movement, were particularly long and detailed and might provide for several alternative courses of action. In the event of difficulties, or breakdowns in communication links, French troops tended to be brought to a standstill, with no possibility for initiative at the local level. It is moving to read, for example, the accounts written by survivors of the Battle of Rossignol of the moment when, on 22 August, an entire French colonial infantry division, cut off from its central command and lacking leadership at the local level, remained immobile, gradually succumbing to enemy fire. Not a single soldier fell back: they were all waiting for their orders. The officers held themselves erect so as to be better seen by their men under fire, and were the first to be killed.[74]

In summary, the Battle of the Frontiers set inexperienced troops against each other in a series of separate engagements. These were encounters where the two adversaries came upon each other while they were both in movement, in converging directions. The better training and greater room for initiative of German troops in the field gave them a significant advantage in these days of battle. Quicker to assume battle position and able to deploy their field artillery faster, they could react more effectively to unexpected events in a type of conflict that was new for everyone on the European front. German troops could take advantage of any opportunities appearing suddenly without first needing to confer with their superiors. In the event of unforeseen difficulties, and there would be many that day, German subalterns, much more easily than their French counterparts, were able to exercise initiative and assume responsibility for a potentially life-saving retreat.

CHAPTER 5

ENTRY INTO WAR

Mobilization in France

Due to the Franco-Russian Alliance, Germany's declaration of war against Russia on 1 August 1914 entailed the immediate entry by France into the conflict. The French Council of Ministers ordered a general mobilization, which took effect on 2 August. In France, general mobilization had long been regarded as an ordeal not certain of success, in human as well as material terms. The response rate likely to be achieved by a national effort of this magnitude was unknown. For years, major political forces on the left, whether socialists committed to their internationalist traditions or revolutionary trade unionists, had announced that they planned actively to oppose a conflict in Europe anticipated by many. Although the assassination of the pacifist member and Socialist leader of the Chamber of Deputies Jean Jaurès on 31 July 1914 in Paris was an isolated act, it reflected the anxiety in nationalist circles concerning the attitude that might be adopted by the socialist left and certain trade-union elements. As it happened, the mobilization was an indisputable popular success. Even if the mood of elation often noted by the press at the time seems to have held less sway than one of sombre determination, nearly all men called to report to their mobilization centres did so immediately.[75] The military authorities had feared a desertion rate of more than 10 per cent, but fewer than 2 per cent of conscripts failed to report for duty on time. In addition, some 350,000 volunteers not subject to mobilization showed up at recruitment centres, while about 3,000 men who had deserted prior to mobilization returned to serve. Encouraged by this patriotic response, Louis Malvy, the French interior minister at the time, decided not to act on the infamous 'Carnet B', the compilation of secret lists kept by police in each *département* of 2,500 known pacifist agitators to be arrested in the event of mobilization. Apart from its popular success, the mobilization also served as an excellent demonstration of the authorities' remarkable technical and administrative capabilities. Through the use of white mobilization posters pasted up in less than twenty-four hours on official noticeboards in every town hall in France, reinforced by notices in daily newspapers with a circulation four times greater than today for a population half as large, the mobilization order reached its target almost instantaneously. Moreover, not only were all conscripts reporting to their different depots able to be immediately equipped and integrated within their units, but those units were very rapidly transferred to their concentration positions along France's north-eastern border. Between 2 and 18 August, 4,278 trains transported the bulk of the French army to the stations of Sedan, Montmédy, Toul, Nancy and Belfort.[76]

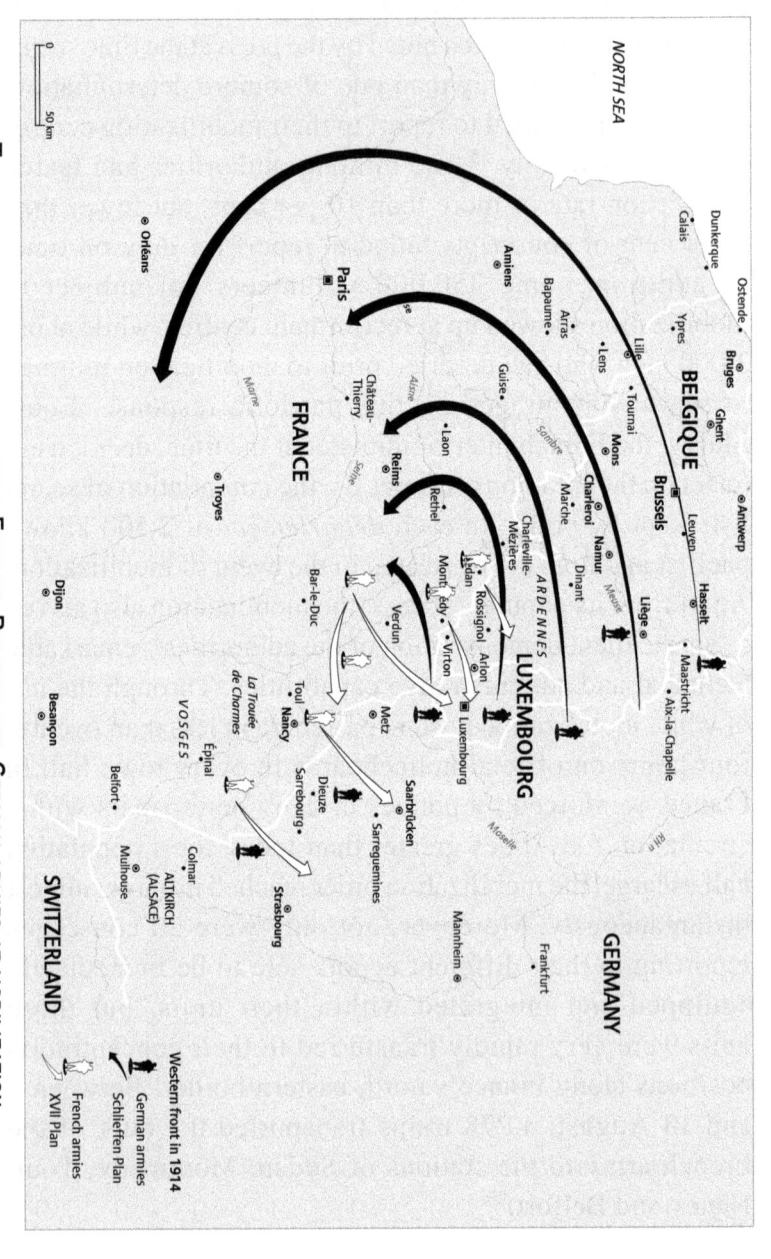

THE CONCENTRATION ZONES OF THE FRENCH, BELGIAN AND GERMAN ARMIES AT MOBILIZATION

In less than two weeks, the peacetime army of 884,000 men absorbed 621,000 reservists into its forty-five infantry divisions, while a further 650,000 men were assigned to twenty-five reserve divisions and another 184,000 were organized into twelve territorial divisions. At the same time, the navy began to transport the colonial divisions based in Algeria and Tunisia across the Mediterranean. Thus a vast force of nearly 1.6 million men, a figure without precedent in the country's history, converged on its regional depots before being directed, in a coordinated fashion, towards north-eastern France. Never in the history of Western Europe had so many men been moved so far in so little time. Conversely, it was clear to everyone that it would not be possible to keep such a large proportion of the male population in service without causing the collapse of a modern economy. The war therefore needed to be short, with its strategy directed towards obtaining a rapid victory.

Other than the soldiers, it is important to mention another 'population', whose mobilization, essential to the war effort, was just as extensive and efficiently accomplished: horses.[77] As was the case for its human citizens, France carried out a yearly census of its equine population in peacetime. All owners of horses, mules and hinnies were required to list their property with a local commission. There were only eleven exemptions, including one relating to horses used by the president of the Republic. In August 1914, of the more than a million horses and mules listed in the census, a total of 610,000 were requisitioned. As a result of battle and poor treatment, about 40 per cent of these animals would die in the war, a mortality rate twice that of the men. Despite progress made in the motorization of armies, requisitions in France would very soon prove inadequate, leading to the importing of horses in massive numbers, mainly from South America.

Mobilization in Germany

In Germany, which had declared war against France on 3 August, an equivalent force was being put in place, in a similar fashion. On the Western Front, the Germans initially mobilized forty-seven active, thirty-three reserve, and three *Landwehr* divisions. The German mobilization compares favourably with that of France in terms of the efficiency of railway transportation. Beginning on 1 August, 560 trains, each consisting of fifty-four carriages and moving at an average speed of thirty kilometres per hour, rolled across the Rhine's bridges on a daily basis. Between 8 and 12 August, the Hohenzollern Bridge in Cologne alone saw the passage of 2,500 trains filled with troops. This was an impressive spectacle: a single army corps (about 40,000 men) was spread over thirty kilometres, its munitions train over twenty kilometres, and the baggage train over a further six kilometres. As in France, plans devised to arrest elements in opposition to the war were discreetly set aside. On 3 August, the German Social Democratic Party caucus voted to grant war credits, with seventy-eight in favour and only fourteen opposed. By the next day, when the caucus voted on a budget of 2.27 billion marks for the first thirty days of mobilization, followed by an immediate supplementary grant of 5 billion, both measures received unanimous approval. The seven German armies were deployed in an arc, with the Seventh Army at the Swiss border in Strasbourg, the Sixth along the Saar, the Fifth outside Metz and the Fourth outside Luxembourg. The German Third Army was to advance through the forest of the Ardennes. The last two armies, with the highest number of troops (320,000 for the First Army and 260,000 for the Second Army), would march into Belgium towards Liège and Namur. The German army thus had to move 600,000 soldiers across the Rhine as quickly as possible, through a corridor only about twenty kilometres wide.

Mobilization in Belgium and Britain

At 7 p.m. on 2 August, the German ambassador to Brussels delivered Germany's ultimatum to Belgium, demanding immediate permission to march its armies through the country to confront what was presented as imminent French aggression. Two hours later, Albert I, king of the Belgians, met with his council of ministers and his general staff to decide upon the proper course of action. The ultimatum was swiftly refused.[78]

It seems that two strategic options for the country's defence had been discussed in this meeting. The first was to concentrate the forces of the Belgian army[79] between Liège and Namur in order to attempt to resist the German assault by relying on the forts surrounding these two cities and the natural barrier created by the Meuse. The aim would have been to hold out for as long as possible while waiting for French, or British, assistance to arrive, as either country was expected to come to the aid of the Belgians rather quickly. But there was a risk that the Belgian army would be completely defeated in the initial fighting and would no longer have the opportunity to seek protection behind Antwerp's forts in the western part of the country to wait for its allies without fully exposing itself to the first German attack. Given the low numerical strength of the Belgian army, and not sure of the time required for reinforcements to arrive, the country's authorities decided in favour of the second option, that is, to wait. For its defence, the Liège garrison thus had to rely on its own forces (mainly local militia members) and its fortifications, built around 1890. Designed to resist the largest-calibre artillery of the period (210 mm), these forts were made of concrete, without any steel framework. They therefore proved no match for the shells fired by 305-mm and 420-mm howitzers.

In London, once the violation of the treaty guaranteeing Belgium's neutrality had been noted, entry into war was automatic. British mobilization was organized in an orderly fashion. The British Expeditionary Force, comprising 130,000 active-duty troops, thus already available and equipped, was dispatched rather quickly to the Continent: five days of convoys in mid-August, under the protection of the Royal Navy, would allow most of these troops to arrive in France. In Great Britain itself, the only logistical difficulties would involve the requisitioning of 120,000 horses and, especially, the reception of tens of thousands of volunteers. The latter, lacking any military experience due to the absence of conscription, would require months to be equipped and trained.

The Battle of Liège

With its ring of twelve forts, six on either bank of the Meuse, and located about thirty kilometres from the French border, the city of Liège provided the first serious obstacle to the advancing German troops. At the very time when the concentration of German reserve troops was being carried out on the other bank of the Rhine and would not be finished before mid-August, the German general staff had planned an immediate assault on the city using its active forces, particularly the 'Army of the Meuse', combining three corps from the Second Army (about 40,000 men under the command of General Otto von Emmich). Beginning on 4 August, only slightly impeded by a few detachments of Belgian cavalry and cyclists, the German troops advanced rapidly towards the city.

In the afternoon of 5 August, a German officer sent as an emissary presented himself before General Gérard Leman, the garrison's commander, demanding permission for the passage of the German forces. As this ultimatum was promptly rejected, the German assault began immediately. It combined the heavy bombardment of the forts with the forward movement of five columns of infantry (two in the north, two in the south and one to the east of the city). Initially, the Belgian forts held up against the shelling. During the confrontations that continued into the night, the Belgian soldiers, hurriedly entrenched between the forts, offered surprising resistance to the German troops. As dawn broke on 6 August, the Germans thus saw their first battle and were forced to retreat following heavy losses. The Second Army commander, General Karl von Bülow, received a message at his headquarters in Hanover, alerting him to the retreat, ascribed to the 'fanatic resistance' of 'Belgian civilians'. This message foreshadowed the future reprisals against these civilians, actions by troops exasperated by this unexpected resistance. These reprisals began with the execution of some twenty prisoners of war and civilians in Herstal, home to the Belgian national arms factory.[80] In the afternoon of 6 August, the Germans renewed their attacks. Determined to continue resistance as long as the forts remained intact, but keen to safeguard what remained of his infantry for future battles, Leman ordered these troops to withdraw in order to join the bulk of the army to the west of Brussels. The forts of Liège were thus isolated from one another and could only be defended individually. Some fell rapidly, in particular the undefended citadel, its surrender boldly secured by General Erich Ludendorff, who had shown up in person with his brigade, and who banged on the main doors with the hilt of his sword, effectively frightening the few Belgian reservists inside. This audacious act helped build Ludendorff's prestige and ensure his rapid ascension within the German military hierarchy.

Having achieved the freedom to manoeuvre around the forts, the assailants were able to transport their largest-calibre field guns, heavy 420-mm howitzers, which could only be moved at an average speed of about two kilometres per hour. Dispatched from the Rhineland, they arrived in position on 12 August. The Belgian forts were not able to withstand such a volume of explosives. The forts of Liège thus began to fall one after another. On 16 August, Fort de Loncin was hit by a shell that exploded in its magazine, thus levelling the entire fort. Sifting through the rubble, the Germans found Leman pinned under a huge block of masonry, alive but unconscious. After reviving him, the assailants carried Leman to General von Emmich, who refused to accept the Belgian general's proffered sword, preserving his military honour. Soon there would be no resistance to the German advance. Far from being taken in forty-eight hours as planned, Liège thus held its own for twelve days against the Germans, who could now move their forces towards Brabant in the west and the Ardennes in the south. In spite of this Belgian resistance, the impact on the timetable of the Schlieffen Plan as adapted by Moltke was minimal. The concentration of German reservists at their departure points in the Rhineland had just been completed. The delay in their forward movement amounted to perhaps forty-eight hours, at most. On the other hand, the German troops, exasperated by this unexpected Belgian resistance as well as casualties due to friendly fire, frequently directed their wrath upon the civilian population.[81]

THE FRENCH RAID INTO ALSACE

From the first week of the war, even though the concentration of French forces in the north-east had yet to run its course, Joffre was keen to carry out rapidly a first offensive military operation. The desired objective was above all political: to show the French people, as well as France's ally Russia, that the French army was entirely ready to initiate hostilities. Joffre instructed General Auguste Dubail, the First Army commander, to enter Alsace from the south, at the level of the Swiss border. This operation, rich in symbolism, was entrusted to General Louis Bonneau, a native Alsatian and the commander of VII Corps. Strictly speaking, given the relatively low number of troops engaged (the 14th and 41st Infantry Divisions together with the 8th Cavalry Division, thus a total of about 20,000 men), this operation should be considered more a raid than an offensive. At dawn on 5 August, these French troops thus left Belfort, advancing into Alsace towards the villages of Altkirch and Thann, along the Swiss border, in the direction of Mulhouse. At Altkirch, the French troops took a German garrison by surprise: its personnel were rapidly routed by a series of bayonet charges, led by young officers, recent Saint-Cyr graduates, wearing plumed shakos and white gloves and backed by cavalry from the eighth regiment of mounted cuirassiers. News of the French success and its first recapture of an Alsatian village, ideally achieved in line with French military doctrine, reached Paris late in the afternoon and prompted a vast wave of popular enthusiasm. However, Bonneau was only to advance towards Mulhouse – his main objective – slowly and cautiously. Lacking updated maps and reliable military information, he was uncertain of the route to follow, not to mention the extent of resistance he was likely to encounter. And yet Mulhouse had been abandoned by the German troops, who had fallen back to a point about twenty kilometres north of the city. But the French would only make their entrance into Mulhouse the next day, at about 3 p.m. Bonneau immediately organized a long parade of French troops, led by soldiers carrying poles used to mark the border with Germany that had been uprooted the previous day, which was received with great enthusiasm by the local population, at least its French-speaking portion. Beginning on 9 August, the German Seventh Army command decided to counter-attack, backed by a very strong artillery contingent. The fighting that night and the next day was intense, not especially well coordinated, and resulted in many casualties on both sides. Shaken by the German counter-attack and especially the intensity of the fighting, Bonneau decided to back down on the evening of 10 August. He would only stop his retreat once his forces had reached the walls of the fort of Belfort – his point of departure – on 13 August. By this time, the population of Mulhouse had fallen again under German control and reprisals were being carried out against the inhabitants who had shown their enthusiasm for France a few days earlier. As for Bonneau, together with his cavalry commander, he would be the first of the French general officers to be relieved of his command. Anthony Clayton sums up the lessons of this French operation as follows:

The whole operation, small-scale though it was, showed up both the ferocity of German firepower and all the weaknesses in the French 1914 military system – incompetent, often elderly commanders, regimental officers too few in number for effective command and with inadequate maps, combat intelligence unreliable or incorrectly evaluated, cavalry steeped in a doctrine of sabre charges rather than reconnaissance, and infantry of reckless bravery but low tactical competence.[82]

Bonneau's command would be entrusted to Pau (who had been passed over in favour of Joffre as chief of the general staff in 1913). Pau renewed the attack on Mulhouse on 18 August and recaptured the city the next day. Following a new counter-attack by the Germans, the French troops abandoned the city on 25 August. They would not set foot there again until the end of the war.

Joffre's strategy

The German army commanders on the Western Front all entered the war in perfect knowledge of their general staff's operational plan (Moltke's version of the Schlieffen Plan). Fully versed in its details, they also enjoyed a certain flexibility in terms of the plan's implementation, provided they conformed to its architecture and its overall philosophy, which had been part of the fibre of their being for some time: the main lines of the Schlieffen Plan had in fact been well established for twenty years.

In contrast, even with the benefit of hindsight, the precise strategy adopted by Joffre after being named commander-in-chief of the French forces has remained, to this day, difficult to pin down. No detailed French operational plan for the war has ever been found. Joffre's secretive nature, his determination to ensure full freedom of choice in all circumstances and, both during and after the war, his reluctance to shoulder responsibility for a catastrophic start to the conflict combined to obscure the actual objectives that might have been pursued by his strategy. However, given the record level of human and materiel losses during the first three weeks of the war, the question of whether, apart from the instructions for the concentration of troops included in Plan XVII, a precise operational plan for the French forces ever existed, and who might have prepared it, deserved an answer. This question would be raised by a parliamentary commission of inquiry, which met in July 1919, chaired by the fiercely independent deputy Maurice Viollette. Its relatively narrow aim was to try to understand why the iron mines of the Briey basin in Lorraine, essential to the war effort, had been relinquished to the enemy so early in the conflict. No conclusion was ever reached by the commission. However, Joffre was compelled to appear. Because his testimony at this hearing is both revealing and instructive, it is included here verbatim:[83]

> CHAIRMAN: Who prepared the operational plan?
> JOFFRE: The army's general staff, under my supervision.
> CHAIRMAN: General de Castelnau has stated under oath that, as deputy chief of the general staff, he had no knowledge of any operational plan.
> JOFFRE: I am not able to say why that might be.
> CHAIRMAN: Who would have prepared the

operational plan and who worked alongside you if the deputy chief did not take part?

JOFFRE: I do not precisely recall these events in enough detail in order to answer you.

CHAIRMAN: Who then took part in the preparation of the operational plan?

JOFFRE: I do not recall.

CHAIRMAN: It seems to me that you should be able to recall the officers with whom you worked; clearly, this must have been a matter of great importance for you.

JOFFRE: But the entire general staff took part. An operational plan is something that you bear in mind, but is never put down on paper!

CHAIRMAN: I would like to make sure that we have understood. For you, an operational plan is something that is kept in mind, but is not put down on paper.

JOFFRE: We write up notes when we want to communicate something in particular to one officer, and something else to another. But there was no prepared plan, as was the case for the concentration plan, for example.

CHAIRMAN: Thus there is nothing on paper. There are no documents at the war ministry that would contain the operational plan?

JOFFRE: I don't think so. There are only guidelines for the concentration.

CHAIRMAN: I must admit that I fail to understand how, for something so important to the country, there can be no trace to be found.

JOFFRE: There might be, perhaps, but I did not write up anything.

CHAIRMAN: All the same, it seems to me that an operational plan should anticipate

various possible scenarios, also foreseeing their repercussions, include a discussion of all means that may be brought to bear by the enemy in response, and also the steps to be taken in order to...
JOFFRE (*interrupting the Chairman*): You're asking me a whole lot of questions on things I know nothing about![84]

And yet, on 3 August, Joffre had met with his five army commanders (Dubail, Castelnau, Ruffey, Langle de Cary and Lanrezac) before they returned to their respective commands. They left the meeting exactly as they had entered it, without any clear information about an overall operational plan, and without precise instructions for the forces under their command. Lanrezac jotted down the following churlish summation in his notes:

> I am more than ever convinced that General Joffre, absolutely dependent upon his general staff officers, will never entertain the opinions of his army commanders, contenting himself with guiding their movements without even indicating the objective he has in mind. It's a Napoleonic system, but only Napoleon could make it work.

Lanrezac had always been a fierce critic of the all-out offensive, and took a dim view of the close relations between Joffre and his young general staff officers, who were all partisans of this approach. The latter were eager to ensure that the 'Napoleonic opportunity' would be seized correctly, when the time came, by army commanders whose prudence they interpreted as faint-heartedness. Hence their interest in shutting out these generals from the strategy formulation process. The most influential among these officers was General Henri Berthelot, given responsibility for the preparation of battle plans. One of Lanrezac's subordinates who had been sent to the Grand Quartier Général (GQG) to argue for a postponement of the offensive that Joffre was preparing to launch in Lorraine in mid-August encountered the famously dogmatic, secretive and hot-headed Berthelot and described the latter's distaste for details as follows:

> I knocked on the door of a study room and whom should I see there but General Berthelot, in his trademark work attire: a skullcap, a white scarf around his neck and a black twill overcoat with baggy, white harem pants and slippers. The room clearly had a dual purpose, serving as his office and his bedroom. From the unmade bed to the chamber pot, everything prompted this conclusion. Seated in armchairs, I spotted General Joffre and General Belin. I left with the very distinct feeling that I had failed across the board in carrying out the main aim of my mission.[85]

On the morning of 8 August, Joffre sent his army commanders his 'General Instruction No. 1'. This document unveiled his overall strategic plan, 'to rush on the enemy with all forces united'. Without offering further details, Joffre urged his army commanders to 'immediately see to the necessary arrangements in order to facilitate the offensive and make sure it delivers a crushing blow'. Joffre thus indicated his intention not to wait passively for a German offensive, but instead to move to attack, at a time yet to be specified, initially by sending the First and Second Armies on his right into Alsace and Lorraine. Expecting the Germans to be attempting to sweep through the plains of Belgium with most of their troops, he seems to have thought that, as a result of this westward movement, the enemy centre would be relatively vulnerable. Thus by quickly launching an offensive thrust he thought it would be possible to tear open this centre (inspired by Napoleon's strategy at Austerlitz) and achieve a decisive victory. And this was of course what the Germans were hoping for: drawing out the French forces so that they would be trapped by the enveloping manoeuvre, the crux of the Schlieffen Plan. At this date, the French general staff was fully aware that, for several days already, the Germans had been laying siege to Liège. But Joffre was convinced that, apart from the troops besieging the citadel, the units having invaded Belgium were mainly cavalry reconnaissance squadrons.

For years, the French had been anticipating a German invasion of Belgium, which would have the immense benefit of bringing Britain into the conflict on their side. This expectation had coloured their own concentration plan, which aimed to give no justification for the long-awaited German aggression. But once this aggression had come to pass, it was viewed with a certain indifference by Joffre and his general staff. Hence there was no immediate movement of troops into Belgium: only General Jean-François Sordet's cavalry corps, consisting of three divisions, was sent into the country on 7 August. It would roam aimlessly, lacking any explicitly defined mission in terms of reconnaissance or contact with the enemy. In the August heat, the cavalry, and especially their horses, would quickly tire of rambling through the countryside in this way.[86] Obtaining information about the enemy, its forces or its intentions did not seem to be a major priority for the French general staff. From this perspective, verging on the negation of reality, it was not considered important to be familiar with the adversary's intentions and manoeuvring capacity since, when faced in battle, the magic of the élan vital would allow the French to rout the enemy by charging with bayonets held high.

Thus, until the end of August, neither Joffre nor his general staff had a clear idea of the extent of the German campaign in Belgium and they also underestimated the number of divisions being deployed against the French left wing. Most importantly, they did not realize that Germany's first-line units had been considerably reinforced with the addition of young and well-trained reservists. Joffre wanted to attack with his armies in Lorraine and Alsace and was fully aware of the risk of his forces being enveloped on the left by the German troops sweeping through Belgium. On 12 August, he thus permitted Lanrezac, the Fifth Army commander, to cross the Belgian border and move his I Corps into the region of Dinant: these troops were to take up position along the Sambre and watch the passages of the Meuse. The troops of the British Expeditionary Force, having landed at ports along the English Channel, would cover Lanrezac's left and advance towards Mons. At the same time, Joffre reinforced his left wing by sending Lanrezac the first divisions arriving from North Africa and those that Italy's declaration of neutrality had permitted to be transferred from south-eastern France. Sordet's cavalry corps, its horses exhausted from their aimless wanderings of the previous days, were also placed under Lanrezac's command. Lastly, Joffre moved Langle de Cary's Fourth Army, which had been kept in reserve until then, in a northerly direction, waiting for the orientation of the German attack to become more apparent. These forces would therefore take up position opposite the Belgian Ardennes, sandwiched between Lanrezac's Fifth Army and Pierre Ruffey's Third Army. Now concluding that his front was sufficiently reinforced on its left flank, Joffre considered that the time was ripe to attack and reconquer Lorraine.

The French offensive in Lorraine

On 14 August, Joffre ordered Dubail's First Army and Castelnau's Second Army to launch an offensive. Joffre's 'General Instruction No. 5' states, with his typical soldierly dash and vagueness, 'The enemy will be attacked wherever it can be found.' In fact, the First Army was to move on Sarrebourg, and the Second on Morhange. The day of the attack had been selected in part to coincide with the launch of the offensive by the Russians on the Eastern Front (the

Russians had been able to mobilize their forces much more quickly than anticipated by the Germans). Lanrezac, whose reconnoitring squadrons had informed him that the enemy was moving through Belgium with forces far greater than had been indicated by GQG, sent word to Joffre, trying to convince him that the major portion of the German effort would be concentrated on the invasion of Belgium. In addition, on 15 August, Lanrezac met with Joffre in a vain attempt to dissuade him from pushing the offensive into Lorraine before the situation had been clarified. Furthermore, that same day, the Germans had crossed the Meuse and then assailed I Corps of Lanrezac's Fifth Army, commanded by Louis Franchet d'Espèrey (later made a Marshal of France), inflicting heavy casualties before being repelled. It was in this battle that, on the outskirts of Dinant, Lieutenant Charles de Gaulle, who was serving in the 33rd Infantry Regiment commanded by Colonel Philippe Pétain, would be wounded for the first time.[87]

On 16 August, it was the turn of the British Expeditionary Force commander John French to seek out Joffre at his Château-Thierry headquarters. Joffre expressed his belief that the main part of the German effort would not be focused on Belgium but more to the east, at the border with Lorraine and Luxembourg. He suggested that French station his troops on Lanrezac's left flank, where his cavalry could be covered by Sordet's corps, and assured him that Lanrezac, whom he praised at length, would be entirely cooperative. Sent at an early age to a Harrow preparatory school, French had followed in his father's footsteps by first joining the Royal Navy, before transferring to the regular army. He found the corpulent and plebeian Joffre very likeable. The next day, he thus decided to pay a visit to Lanrezac, at his Rethel headquarters. French found this meeting far less pleasant than his encounter with Joffre. Although a highly competent general, Lanrezac was a rigid nationalist and ecumenically xenophobic (he found anyone not French barely tolerable). Thus it was hardly surprising that Lanrezac did not welcome this quintessentially British superior officer too warmly, perceiving, and perhaps not wrongly so, French's appearance, general attitude and elegant befuddlement as smacking of condescension. This was only compounded by translation difficulties (the two men had refused to use an interpreter in the interest of security), and the meeting, which had got off to a rough start, ended in even worse shape.[88] The two men came away from their encounter with a mutual and profound feeling of annoyance, which would not be without consequence for Lanrezac: his failure to coordinate with the British Expeditionary Force would be the main reason, at least among those made public, for his *limogeage* the following month. However, these two intelligent men both drew pertinent conclusions from their conversation, despite its unfriendly tone. French understood that Lanrezac did not in any way share Joffre's vision of the German battle plan and ascertained that the Fifth Army commander was very likely better informed of actual developments in the field. As for Lanrezac, the experience only confirmed the determinations he had reached on the basis of his prejudices: if things took a turn for the worse, there was no point in expecting the British Expeditionary Force to get cut down covering an eventual French retreat rather than moving quickly to re-embark.[89]

Opposite the two French armies were the German Sixth and Seventh Armies, both under the command of Crown Prince Rupprecht of Bavaria. The German tactic was simple: in the face of the French advance that they fully expected and welcomed because it would facilitate their envelopment movement via the west, the Germans began by ceding ground, drawing the French troops further to the north. Rearguard actions, especially the use of long-range artillery, aimed simply to slow down the French advance. In Lorraine, as distinct from Belgium, the German armies were moving on familiar terrain, in land they had occupied for forty-four years. Above all, these were areas where, quite intentionally, they had been drilling their troops for years and their artillery positions had been in place for a long time. For example, near the village of Dieuze on 19 August, the soldiers of the Second Army's XV Corps would find themselves venturing precisely upon one of these very drill grounds.[90] Jean-Yves Le Naour describes how these French troops advanced without encountering any resistance at the outset, on a flat terrain, punctuated at regular intervals by large grooved poles.[91] They were unaware, in the absence of any information from military intelligence, that they were moving on a drill ground belonging to the enemy: the poles were used for distance-adjustment purposes during long-range exercises by the German artillery (whose officers certainly were observing them at the same moment through their binoculars). When they determined the moment had come to do so, the German artillery began firing. The soldiers of the French Second Army would thus be among the first twentieth-century combatants to experience the impact of a modern artillery barrage.

Apart from direct fatalities due to shell blasts, the effect of the barrage was devastating even to those soldiers not hit directly: mucous membranes (tympanum, sphincter) in particular were very vulnerable to this onslaught. No troops, moving across open terrain, have ever been able to hold their positions under this type of bombardment.[92] XV Corps, its numbers decimated, began pulling back in a state of some disarray the following day, 20 August, when the Germans launched a general counter-attack in Lorraine.[93] Until this date, the French First and Second Armies had advanced slowly but methodically for five days, facing German troops that did not dispute the ground. The First Army had reached Sarrebourg, which had been evacuated by the Germans, and the Second was in sight of Morhange. But there had been heavy losses. Germany's long-range artillery had pounded the advancing French troops, whose 75-mm field guns did not have the range necessary to form an effective counter-battery. In particular, the German rearguard, well installed in positions prepared in advance and abundantly covered by machine-gun fire, had inflicted heavy casualties on French units, who had charged the German positions with bayonets. Already on the second day of the offensive, Castelnau, the Second Army's commander, had informed Joffre of the failure, plain for all to see at that point, of the French all-out-attack tactic.[94] In his report, Castelnau had insisted upon the need, when coming upon entrenched defensive positions, to better prepare the attacks, particularly through the use of artillery, rather than rushing on the enemy troops, accompanied by bugle calls, as soon as they were spotted. Joffre and his general staff, content to see that the troops were advancing and that the enemy was retreating, would be unfazed by these initial warnings.

The German counter-offensive of 20 August, massively supported by artillery, proved to be particularly violent. The Second Army's XX Corps, commanded by Foch, bore the brunt of the attack outside Morhange. In contrast to the Germans, the French troops had not been trained in the procedure for quickly setting up protected defensive positions, which would have run counter to French military doctrine of the period. The withdrawal would therefore be carried out in a highly disorganized fashion, in open terrain, under fire, thus resulting in heavy losses.[95] It would lead to the retreat of the entire Second Army, followed by the First Army, which had to evacuate Sarrebourg, conquered for the French not long before.[96] The French troops quickly went back across the 1871 border, pursued by the Germans. The French offensive to liberate Lorraine was thus transformed into the defence of Nancy, one of the country's main fortified sites, along with Toul and Verdun. Foch, whose XX Corps was comprised fittingly of soldiers from Lorraine, succeeded in turning the situation to the French advantage at the Grand Couronné, just outside Nancy. From 24 August, Rupprecht, buoyed by his success, began to entertain the notion that his Sixth and Seventh Armies could win the war on their own, in opposition to Germany's strategic plan, according to which his role was intended to be purely defensive. Rupprecht's forces rushed into the Charmes Gap (the narrow corridor between Toul and Verdun), only to be foiled once again by Foch's troops. Battle then continued on the outskirts of Nancy, with successive attacks and counter-attacks, but without any significant results until mid-September, when both sides began to dig into their trenches, where they were to continue to hold out for nearly four more years.

THE ARDENNES OFFENSIVE

On 18 August, to round out his offensive movement, Joffre initially ordered Ruffey's Third Army and Langle de Cary's Fourth Army to move to the north of their respective positions. However, he held the troops back for two more days for fear, it seems, of attacking too early. Since the start of the war, the French general staff, failing to understand the impact of the integration of Germany's reservists with its first-line units, had consistently underestimated the enemy troops, in terms of both strength and number. Having received many reports on the growing numbers of German troops crossing the Meuse and pouring into western Belgium,[97] Joffre therefore concluded that the Germans could only be achieving this movement by fatally thinning out their centre, on the border of Belgium and Luxembourg. Joffre thus waited until the evening of 20 August, the day when the Germans launched their counter-offensive in Lorraine, to give the order to advance into the Ardennes. The German counter-offensive in Lorraine strengthened his conviction that the German centre was certainly only defended by a smattering of troops and would hence be very vulnerable. In the interim, Joffre had modified the composition of his forces in several ways: he transferred two additional corps to the Fourth Army – XI Corps, originally with the Fifth Army and under Lanrezac's command, and IX Corps, originally with the Third Army – as its role was becoming critical in breaking through the German forces. The mission of this new, larger Fourth Army was to cross the Semois, which forms the border with Belgium, and advance towards Neufchâteau. As for the Third Army, it would be split in two: a portion of these forces, renamed as the 'Army of Lorraine', would be placed under the command of Michel Joseph Maunoury, a general called from retirement (he was sixty-seven years old), with the aim of providing cover for the Second Army, which had begun to fall back towards Nancy, while defending the region of Verdun. The remainder of the Third Army, under Ruffey, was to advance towards Arlon, in Luxembourg, while protecting the right flank of the Fourth Army against a German counter-attack.

On 21 August, the newly reorganized French troops began advancing slowly towards Belgium, through a series of marches and counter-marches that tired out the enlisted men and the officers, under heavy rains blanketing the entire region. The troops lacked the appropriate maps and had little up-to-date information, but morale was good. That day, they would encounter only a handful of German cavalry patrols, thus confirming the messages received from GQG, according to which they should expect to run up against just a few Uhlans. But the following fateful day would bring with it the bloody realization that eastern Belgium was far from being nearly empty of German troops: instead, they were assuredly present in greater numbers than the French forces.

Lanrezac's advance towards Namur and Charleroi

On 20 August, Joffre had asked Lanrezac to move his Fifth Army more to the north, in Belgium, to cross the Sambre and hold a defensive position between Namur and Charleroi. If the Fourth Army was successful in making an opening on its right, the Fifth Army's role would be to join up with it to form a pincer movement around the invading German forces, or else to combine its forces with those of the Belgian army, concentrated around Antwerp, to stop the Germans from advancing westward. Lanrezac was becoming increasingly concerned, despite the arrival of reinforcements in the form of three reserve divisions, about the size of the German forces that he would have to face, estimating that they were twice as strong in number as his own. With respect to their advance, he would rather have been moving forward for several days already, before too many Germans entered the north of Belgium, and he was afraid that now it was too late. In fact, he had the clear impression that an envelopment battle was looming and wanted to avoid rushing into a trap that could lead to the encircling and subsequently the destruction of his army. There were fifteen divisions in Lanrezac's army, not including the British Expeditionary Force taking up position on his left flank, while the two German armies heading in his direction together had thirty-eight. On 21 August, Lanrezac thus tried to stop his various units from advancing, but his orders would not be received, or would not be carried out, by ambitious generals. On the morning of 21 August, the first elements of the German Second Army under General von Bülow encountered the French forces at the Sambre, which they had managed to cross at several points, thus commencing the Battle of Charleroi.

At dawn on 22 August 1914, the French army found itself in an exceptional situation. Three weeks after the general mobilization, all of the Republic's forces were actively engaged in battle, or would soon be. And over a front 400 kilometres long, stretching from the Swiss border to the Brabant in Belgium. That day, from east to west along this front, hundreds of thousands of men would see combat in fifteen major battles, a phenomenon entirely without precedent. It would never be repeated throughout the remainder of the war, because the front would never again be so completely ablaze with battle from one end to the other. Furthermore, in contrast to the circumstances at play for most of the conflict, troops would here be facing each other in a war of movement, thus chiefly over open terrain, without the benefit of well-coordinated trenches or fortifications. This fact would make the carnage on that day all the more dreadful.

CHAPTER 6

THE BATTLE OF THE ARDENNES

On 22 August, the six corps of the French Fourth Army crossed into Belgium.[98] From east to west, IX Corps (with troops from the region of Tours), XI Corps (Nantes), XVII Corps (Toulouse), the Colonial Corps, XII Corps (Limoges) and II Corps (Amiens),[99] organized in separate columns, advanced through the forest of the Ardennes, moving towards a line about forty kilometres long extending from Givet in the west to Virton in the east. These six corps were arrayed so that each unit was slightly out of alignment with the others, thus moving forward in oblique order or echelon formation. The aim was to use the advance of the next army corps to protect the right flank of the previous one. Ruffey's Third Army advanced northward from Virton towards Longwy, with two army corps (IV Corps and V Corps), while VI Corps was to take up a protective position near Longwy. With this strategy, Joffre sought to attack the German flank advancing from east to west in Belgium. This was a catastrophic error. In fact, the German armies had already turned southward and were thus on a path that would lead to confrontation with the French troops. On 22 August, nearly all of the French army corps would thus find themselves engaged in intense fighting against units of the German Fourth Army (under Albrecht, Duke of Württemberg) and its Fifth Army (under Crown Prince Wilhelm of Prussia), both arriving from the north, with varying results. The day's main battle sites – Virton, Ethe, Bellefontaine, Rossignol, Neufchâteau, Ochamps, Bertrix and Maissin – are situated along an arc bisecting the Belgian province of Luxembourg, bordered to the east by the grand duchy of the same name.

In nature, no battle is ever entirely like another. However, the day's various engagements share several striking characteristics. The analysis given in the second chapter of the bloodiest of these battles (at least for the French), which saw the annihilation of two Colonial Corps divisions outside the village of Rossignol, sheds light on all of them. Without entering into the details of the movements of each unit, it is interesting to review briefly, from east to west, the particulars of the day's events, and the main characteristics they have in common.

First of all, they are all battles of encounter. At nearly every occasion on 22 August, the adversaries were surprised to find themselves face to face with one another. There are a number of reasons why this was the case, beginning with issues specific to the terrain at hand. In this undulating, wooded region, cut through by winding streams and rivers, the harsh relief meant that there were few sites from which one might have been able to obtain a clear view over any sizeable distance. Furthermore, as mentioned earlier, heavy rains had blanketed the entire region the previous day. It was hot and sticky at dawn, and the thick fog on the morning of 22 August would only clear by around noon. On the French side, information relayed about the movement of enemy troops would be insufficient, and frequently imprecise. The French army's headquarters had reported that most of the German troops were still between one and two days' march away. On 22 August, the French troops thus only expected to run up against German cavalry patrols on reconnaissance missions. In 1914, it was possible to obtain information through air observation, but only in a very primitive manner. Pilots only flew by day and in good weather. As a result, their planes remained mostly on the ground throughout the day on 21 August and on 22 August in the morning. A pilot who wanted to communicate the results of an observation had first to find a field where he could land; then he needed to contact the proper military commander (himself on the move behind his troops) in order to deliver this information, whose recipient was of course fully accountable for making appropriate use of it. Given these circumstances, most of the information-gathering tasks were carried out by the cavalry, who as a general rule, hardly relished this role, much preferring the prospect of charging the enemy, and preferably other cavalrymen. In addition, the cavalry units were only rarely equipped with maps of the Ardennes, since it was never imagined that they would be engaged in battle in the forest. Lastly, units often used information provided by Belgian civilians, who proved to be highly cooperative with the French troops, but who had only a partial, and often contradictory, perspective on enemy movements.

In fact, the French Third and Fourth Armies pushed blindly into the Ardennes, completely in the dark about their adversary's positions or its strength.

The first observation we can make on reading the many accounts surviving into the present day penned by veterans of the Battle of the Ardennes is that the soldiers and officers due to fight that day were already exhausted. It is true that the order to advance, initially given to the Fourth Army by Joffre on 18 August, had been suspended soon thereafter until the evening of 20 August. However, while waiting for their definitive orders, the troops had not remained immobile. In the August heat, they went on a series of marches and counter-marches, all of them carrying on their backs the maximum weight of kit for the early days of a campaign, sometimes as much as forty kilograms, with their share of battle ammunition. The march forward had begun on 21 August, under a torrential downpour. Given the objectives to be reached on 22 August, the men departed well before dawn, having managed only a few hours of sleep at most. Many of the accounts relate that the precipitous departure had taken place before the men (or the horses) had even been able to get a bite to eat. On this point, the 22 August entry in the personal journal of Jean Moreau, the 3rd Colonial Infantry Division's principal staff officer, is particularly illuminating:

> The wake-up call came at about 2 a.m. An order to prepare to move forward had come from the army corps. The division was to be billeted at Neufchâteau. Our advance guard was to cross the bridge at Mesnil–Breuvannes at 6.30 [...] The order from the army corps offered no new information about the enemy troops, but it recommended that we attack them wherever we would find them. This phrase left us perplexed [...] And we set off while it was still dark, at around 4.15. Before I mounted my horse, I managed to down a bit of a rusk and a few sips of dreadful coffee. En route, I munched on a chocolate bar I found in my pocket [...] The three squadrons of the Sixth Dragoons marched a few hundred metres ahead of us. These poor dragoons, who had been assigned to us only the previous night, had arrived dog-tired and without maps. We were only hearing about this now, surprised at seeing them take the wrong turn at every intersection.[100]

Almost every time, French and German forces met up following a chance encounter (often between two cavalry patrols), and the capacity for improvisation of the German units was shown to be infinitely superior to that of the French, in marked contrast with national stereotypes. Information was relayed much more quickly through the German hierarchy, facilitated by the fact that, due to the warnings provided by their Uhlans, they often fully expected to come up against French troops. German troops were far more efficient at getting into battle – and therefore firing – positions than their French counterparts. Time often lost early in the day, due to indecision within the command structure and inappropriate tactical plans, would compel the French troops, from mid-morning onwards, to manoeuvre under enemy fire, particularly that rained down by German artillery.

Any infantry division in 1914, whether German or French, moving forward on a narrow route through the Ardennes with men (in columns of four across), horses and artillery wagons, ammunition and various equipment, would be spread out over ten to fifteen kilometres, depending on whether the column managed to remain in tight formation. Shifting from a column formation, extending over ten kilometres or more, to a defensive line most often perpendicular to the head of the column at the moment of the encounter with the enemy was a mechanical manoeuvre that required quite a bit of time. The German organizational approach, which left considerable initiative to subalterns and non-commissioned officers, made quick reactions possible, even in the event of a chance encounter. Their infantry took up protected firing positions, making use of the existing terrain (woods, ditches and so on) or quickly digging embankments (rather than true trenches) thanks to their abundant supply of shovels (with which the French troops were only meagrely supplied, since they were expected to mount an attack rather than dig in). Next, the Germans immediately worked on getting their artillery into firing position, often from sites on the downward slopes of hills, difficult to reach for French artillery, which was limited to direct firing due to the characteristics of its 75-mm field gun.

In striking contrast, on the French side, very frequently the nature of the obstacle encountered was completely misunderstood at the outset. In Rossignol, for example, the shots greeting French cavalry chasing the Uhlans encountered in the village into the forest of Neufchâteau were thought to be protective fire laid down by dismounted German cavalry. Furthermore, the French tactical response was always the conventional one: no additional reconnaissance, no precautionary deployment of artillery. An infantry regiment was sent out first, bayonets at the ready, to charge at the obstacle. And when it failed, another was sent, and then another. Lastly, a French tendency towards command paralysis under fire must be acknowledged. Apart from individual failings, such as that of General Raffenel, who experienced a nervous breakdown, the French system of command and communication in August 1914 seems to have been particularly ill suited to the fighting. The halting flow of information from the line of fire to the upper echelons of the hierarchy, followed by the time required to pass along the orders given in the opposite direction, were inappropriate for a war of movement where the positions of each side were constantly changing (as was the general situation). When it was necessary to manoeuvre and command under German artillery fire, which began raining down usually about an hour after the initial contact, the mobility of the French units quickly decreased. Gradually separated from each other by their difficulty in communicating under intense fire, they tended to remain stuck in position, exposed to enemy fire, due to a lack of equipment, but especially the lack of training in taking a defensive stance, which would have run counter to French tactical dogma. Therefore, French soldiers most often remained out in the open, trying sometimes to hide behind their (albeit relatively large) kit.

The final paradox of the day for the French side was that despite the large number of units advancing very close to one another in parallel lines, each of them had to wage battle alone when ultimately clashing with enemy troops.[101] The topographical features of the region, the inadequacies of the system of communication between units in the field, the complex hierarchy of the general staff, the near simultaneity of the start of fighting in the region as a whole and the dissipation of morning fog, and the general disorganization once the troops were under enemy artillery fire combined to prevent the various army corps from coming to each other's aid.

THE THIRD ARMY'S ENCOUNTERS ON 22 AUGUST

The Third Army had been ordered to advance towards Arlon, on the border between Belgium and Luxembourg. On its left, the role to be served by IV Corps was above all to protect the Fourth Army, whose II Corps made up its right flank. Information reaching these forces on 21 August was pithy but precise: 'The region of Virton–Arlon seems to be unoccupied.' Unfortunately, this assessment was incorrect. The Germans had reached a line between Virton and Ethe the day before, less than ten kilometres from the French positions on the evening of 21 August. It was on the outskirts of these two villages that IV Corps's two infantry divisions, the 8th at Virton and the 7th at Ethe, would find themselves in intense and deadly combat all day long.

Setting out at 4 a.m., the 7th Infantry Division's men had no time for the morning meal. In order to move forward more quickly, and since it was thought that they would not be seeing any fighting that day, the ammunition from the supply wagon was not distributed. Each soldier left camp only with his individual ration of eighty-eight cartridges. The French troops had been billeted on the night of 21 August at Ruelles, just four kilometres from the village of Ethe, where the Germans had already arrived. Like most of the villages in the region, Ethe is located at the bottom of a deep valley, hewn by the river Ton. The French cavalrymen of the 14th Hussars, led by Lieutenant Colonel Wallerand de Hauteclocque,[102] were the first to enter Ethe. As at Rossignol, these cavalrymen were mowed down by fire when exiting the village. But in this battle, the German troops, already firmly positioned on the high plateaus overlooking Ethe from the east and west, immediately went on the offensive. By mid-morning, under the lingering and thick cover of fog, they gained a foothold in the village, where the fighting would continue throughout the entire day.

There were heavy losses on both sides, but the situation became increasingly difficult for the French troops, who found themselves surrounded by late afternoon. However, the Germans had neither the time nor the energy on this occasion to complete their pincer movement before nightfall. At around 6 p.m., they fell back to a position beyond the range of French artillery fire. Once darkness had descended, the French 7th Infantry Division, or what was left of it, managed to break through the encircling enemy forces, guided by a German deserter from Hanover who had rejected Prussian militarism and was living in exile in Ethe. Transferred to Paris by rail, the 7th Infantry Division would return to service two weeks later. A portion of these troops would be among those famously shuttled to the Marne battlefields by Parisian taxis. And yet, in the five military cemeteries around Ethe and the neighbouring village of Bleid, there are headstones marking the graves of 2,056 French soldiers.[103]

The 8th Infantry Division, on the 7th Division's left flank, arrived in Virton. Nestled in the next valley, Virton, like Ethe, is dominated by the Robelmont plateau, where the hamlet of Belle-Vue is situated. It was around this hamlet, from the early hours and under cover of heavy fog, that the opposing forces stumbled upon one another and the battle began. Here again, relying on erroneous information from their general staff, the French troops had been spread out in long lines. As always, intelligence filtering down to, and between, French units was woefully inadequate. One after the other, they would be entirely surprised to find themselves under enemy fire once they reached the road leading to Étalle, the objective assigned to the division. The French advance guard fell back to the village where the rest of the column was continuing to arrive, creating congestion and confusion in the extreme. At around 6.30 a.m., the Germans took up positions on the Robelment plateau overlooking the village, which they were getting ready to attack later in the morning. However, the German general staff slowed the advance of its troops once they realized that French troops were marching towards the villages of Bellefontaine and Meix-devant-Virton on the other side of the hill. These were units of the Fourth Army's II Corps. This was the only time during the day that a French army corps came to the aid of another, although indirectly, as the two French units were entirely unaware of their respective positions.

German indecisiveness thus gave the French time to prepare their artillery, after having found a group of spots to place well-protected batteries within the village amid the ruins of the Saint-Joseph convent. All day long, the Germans would have difficulty pinpointing French firing positions and were thus prevented from entering Virton by French artillery units. This fateful twenty-second day of August would subsequently see several successive assaults – and setbacks – with heavy losses on both sides. The Germans, perched safely on high ground, were able to prevent the French from taking the Robelmont plateau. Although less well organized from a defensive standpoint, the French, with the support of their artillery, managed against all odds to prevent the Germans from entering Virton. At around 7.30 p.m., nearly simultaneously, bugles on both sides sounded the ceasefire. Both French and German troops were completely exhausted. At 8 p.m., the French batteries fired a final salvo the aim of which, in the words of General Victor Boëlle, commander of the 8th Infantry Division, was to 'let these people know that the battlefield was ours'. Perhaps, but by 9 p.m., the withdrawal of the French troops had begun, under cover of darkness. The 8th Infantry Division fell back upon Harnoncourt, its point of departure the previous day. With 5,000 dead, wounded and missing, it had lost nearly half of its effective force and more than half of its officers.

II Corps's encounters on 22 August

On the extreme right of the Fourth Army's line, II Corps's mission was above all to cover the Colonial Corps's right flank, which was to reach Neufchâteau that day. But it would not be able to fulfil this role. In fact, given that Montmédy, its starting point, was already considerably to the south of Colonial Corps's point of departure, the latter corps's columns would remain unprotected on their right all day long, thus facilitating their envelopment later in the day. In the meantime, at about 6.30 a.m., II Corps, which had only a single route available to push northward, reached the village of Bellefontaine, which had already been occupied by the Chasseurs d'Afrique since the previous day. The next objective was to reach Tintigny, northwest of Virton. The cavalrymen warned of the presence of German troops in the woods between the two villages. In fact, the German 11th Infantry Division had arrived there the previous day. Reconnaissance patrols had informed this division's commander of the progress made by II Corps, whose advance guard, the 4th Infantry Division, marched in the direction of Tintigny and were met with heavy

German fire along the way. These French troops had to fall back quickly towards Bellefontaine to set up defensive positions. The Germans began attacking Bellefontaine at 9 a.m., an encounter marked by especially violent fighting, which would continue throughout the day. In the meantime, II Corps received a request from the Colonial Corps to provide aid on its left to the 3rd Colonial Infantry Division, in danger of being enveloped at Rossignol. But II Corps was unable to assist as it was trying in vain to push back the German assaults near Bellefontaine. By 2 p.m., the German troops had reached Bellefontaine itself, from where their artillery could fire directly on the French positions. The French foot soldiers withdrew to the centre of the village and set up barricades. The fighting continued, sometimes hand to hand, until about 5 p.m., with the French virtually surrounded but still holding the centre of the village. At this point, the Germans, exhausted from their offensive, which had begun at 9 a.m., decided to fall back to the village of Saint-Vincent rather than continue fighting in Bellefontaine after sundown. Just as exhausted, the French did not follow in their pursuit, but in contrast decided to fall back to their starting point after nightfall.

XVII Corps and the encounters at Bertrix and Ochamps, and in the forest of Luchy

The objective assigned to this army corps, with its two divisions, the 33rd and the 34th, both based in south-western France, was to reach the village of Ochamps. Early in the morning, XVII Corps's advance guard reached their initial objective, the village of Bertrix, about ten kilometres from Ochamps. The locals warned the French command that the forest of Luchy, traversed by the road leading to Ochamps, was teeming with German soldiers. This warning was not heeded. Two infantry regiments, the 11th and the 20th, moved forward with the divisional artillery. As was the case elsewhere in the region, the artillery's advance was made difficult by a narrow and cluttered route, a veritable jumble of guns and wagons. Upon entering the forest of Luchy, the French troops were attacked by the artillery of the German 21st Infantry Division, which had been stationed just outside Ochamps. Unable to manoeuvre under fire, some of the artillerymen were compelled to flee, leaving their guns to the Germans. The remainder managed to find a path cutting through the forest and began to escape along with their guns, but, as it happened, this route was in view of the German artillery, who thus wiped out nearly all of these men, and their equipment, as they withdrew. Once most of the artillery had been either taken or destroyed, the French infantrymen found themselves completely unprotected and exposed to enemy fire for the rest of the day. When attempting to push back the German troops on the outskirts of Ochamps, the French infantry were thwarted by barbed-wire fences since they were not equipped with wire cutters.[104] Over the course of the day, the 20th and 11th Infantry Regiments, both based in Montauban (Tarn-et-Garonne), would lose half of their men.[105] By late afternoon, the sorely tried men of XVII Corps beat a retreat to their base of operations.

XI Corps and the Battle of Maissin

By 7 a.m., the cavalry supporting the 22nd Infantry Division had reached Maissin. But they discovered that German troops already occupied the village and had to fall back, leaving Maissin to the Germans. Later in the morning, the 19th Infantry Regiment, the 22nd Division's advance guard, arrived in the woods of Haumont, about 400 metres from the village. Without waiting for reinforcements to arrive, without preparing the artillery (which had yet to reach their location), the 19th Infantry Regiment began the charge, flags unfurled, pounding their drums and sounding their bugles. Under a heavy rain of fire from German machine guns and Krupp 77-mm field guns (which were already in position, unlike their French counterparts), the regiment met with disaster at the southern entrance to the village. The fighting continued throughout the day. By late afternoon, with the arrival of the rest of the division to provide support, Maissin was captured by the French with a final bayonet charge at around 7 p.m. However, this final effort proved to be in vain: during the night, the XI Corps commander General Joseph-Paul Eydoux, aware that the other French army corps had thrown in the towel, decided that all units should retreat to the previous day's starting positions.

In less than seventy-two hours, the French offensive in the Ardennes was thus revealed as an utter failure: two armies found themselves pushed back to their line of departure on 21 August. In the interim, they had suffered heavy losses. At each section of the front, at nearly every encounter, the weaknesses of the French army in 1914 were flagrant: a disdain for information, inadequate reconnaissance, poorly adapted equipment (uniforms far too brightly coloured, lack of shovels), artillery at a disadvantage in hilly terrain since it was unable to target positions on downward slopes, an excessively long and hierarchical chain of command, mediocre coordination between adjacent units, and so on. Despite all of these shortcomings, the French troops and their officers nevertheless demonstrated, on nearly every occasion, exceptional drive and courage. Everywhere they moved into battle at a rapid pace, in spite of their fatigue. With enthusiasm, they obeyed frequent, repeated and often ill-considered attack orders. Even under heavy fire, in most cases they firmly held their positions, very often far beyond what might reasonably have been expected of them.

In 1922, the French war ministry began the publication of an immense series (106 volumes in all, with maps and appendices) entitled *Les armées françaises dans la Grande Guerre*. Military operations are copiously detailed on a day-to-day basis, with reference to the orders and communications on file, which are included in the appendices. As for all of the fighting during the war, the Battle of the Ardennes is meticulously recounted, unit by unit, site by site, hour after hour. But the chapter closes, in a manner rarely used elsewhere in the series, with two short pages under the terse heading 'Conclusions sur la bataille des Ardennes'. The authors, an unidentified group of writers, refer to the surprise experienced by French units in encountering German troops and mention the inadequate nature of the communication links between them. The closing sentence of this chapter, describing what was, in so many ways, one of the bloodiest catastrophes ever to have struck the French army, is a masterpiece of understatement:

> The result was a set of separate, and to all intents and purposes unrelated, engagements during which neither the general in charge nor the army commanders were able to make their influence felt, but which saw the troops giving their utmost and demonstrating great steadfastness under fire.[106]

In other words, there was nothing Joffre and his generals might have done, and their men were at least able to show that they knew how to get themselves killed.

In fact, what the fighting in the Ardennes made irrefutably clear was the fundamental failure of the doctrine of the all-out offensive. In 1914, firepower always gained the upper hand over courage... and firepower kills.

CHAPTER 7

THE BATTLE OF CHARLEROI AND THE RETREAT

From the German perspective, despite the heavy losses sustained by French troops in the Ardennes on 22 August, the decisive battle still needed to be waged, and won. The Schlieffen Plan, as modified by Moltke, called for a right wing (the German First, Second and Third Armies commanded by Alexander von Kluck, Karl von Bülow and Max von Hausen, respectively) replete with men and equipment reflecting its critical importance. Its role was to ensure victory by means of a decisive battle, in accordance with Prussian strategic doctrine. A victory that, by bringing the maximum impact at a precise place and time, would break the back of the French forces. To Lanrezac's credit, he never let his army play the role of sacrificial victim. His refusal to buy into the brazen folly advocated by prevailing French military doctrine led him to order the retreat of his troops so that they would not be wiped out on the battlefield. Lanrezac would arrive at this decision to withdraw from the engagement without consulting Joffre or the commander-in-chief's general staff, or even his British ally, in position on his left flank. He would thus maintain his army's battle capacity, allowing him to lead rearguard attacks that would slow the German advance and prevent the envelopment of French forces. Furthermore, this decision would give the French time to reassemble troops, in less than two weeks, on a defensive line at the Marne. Not surprisingly, it would cost Lanrezac his military career and (in part at least) his reputation.

On 20 August, Lanrezac had moved his troops to hold a line along the Sambre. He had four army corps, arrayed from east to west: Louis Franchet d'Espèrey's I Corps, Henri Sauret's III Corps, Gilbert Defforges's X Corps and Jacques de Mas-Latrie's XVIII Corps. The British Expeditionary Force, having just landed at the ports along the English Channel, would normally have taken up position on his left. In the meantime, the Fifth Army's left flank was being covered by Sordet's cavalry corps, which had already been roaming the countryside in Belgium for three weeks. To these troops were added the two reserve divisions under the command of General Mardochée Valabrègue. It should not be forgotten that, in French military organization, reserve divisions consisted of territorial units and thus of men around forty years of age. These units were generally not considered suited to a first-line engagement against active German units.

In all, Lanrezac had fifteen divisions at his disposal (including the territorial units, but not counting the three British divisions). Joffre and his entire general staff believed that the Fifth Army would be up against an equivalent number of German divisions. But Lanrezac did not trust this estimate. Moreover, he was not inclined to rely on anything coming from Joffre or his staff: maps, ideas or, in this case, intelligence. As it happens, Lanrezac was completely right to doubt Joffre's figures: with a total of thirty-eight divisions, the three German armies that he would be required to face in fact included twice as many combatants as his Fifth Army.

On 20 August, German troops entered Brussels, without any resistance from the Belgian army, which fell back to Antwerp. Lanrezac readied his forces. On his right, Franchet d'Espèrey's I Corps were to hold the banks of the Meuse, opposite Hausen's Third Army. III Corps and X Corps had moved to the north and were to hold a line between Namur and Charleroi, the two main cities of Belgium's Borinage mining region that Bülow's Second Army was preparing to attack. Mas-Latrie's XVIII Corps was on his left. The corps of reservists, as was customary for territorial units, was positioned at the far western edge and at the rear of the line, covering the region of Maubeuge.

On 21 August, the German Second Army launched a massive attack on Namur and Charleroi, while, further to the east, units of the German Third Army managed to cross the Meuse at various points. They had taken advantage of the many bridges in this densely populated region that had been left either unguarded or guarded by inadequate resources. This highly urbanized area, with its many factories and spoil heaps, facilitated infiltrations by assailants in large numbers. Conversely, defensive forces had the advantage of being able to fire from multiple sheltered positions. Over the next three days, the French and the Germans would alternate attacks and counter-attacks, with both sides sustaining heavy losses.

Faced with the German thrust, Lanrezac hesitated in selecting the appropriate tactic: defending the line between Charleroi and Namur as well as the banks of the Meuse at all costs or taking evasive action and pulling back to the French border. Like Liège, Namur is a city surrounded by forts that the Belgians initially chose to defend. But the example of Liège showed that even when defended with conviction, these fortifications would not be able to hold out for a long time under shelling by German heavy artillery. Lanrezac was well aware that his centre had advanced very far to the north. He knew that he was being attacked on three sides by three German armies and that the Germans were trying to outflank him on his right and envelop his men. As it happened, his left comprised the British Expeditionary Force together with the French territorial units. Lanrezac felt he could not rely on either of these forces to go up against Kluck's First Army. While he hesitated, and without receiving specific orders from Joffre, his commanders, particularly those of III Corps and X Corps, took the initiative to go on the offensive on 22 August. These French counter-attacks would be disastrous for the troops committed. South of Liège, at Tamines and Arsimont, in especially bloody encounters, French soldiers clashed with German troops trying to cross the Sambre. The strength of the assault compelled the French forces to pull back. As in the Ardennes with the Colonial Corps, some of the attacks in open fields, without any cover from French artillery, culminated in the near destruction of elite French regiments. Outside Charleroi, units of Zouaves riflemen and sharpshooters, constituting the majority of the 37th Infantry Division, were decimated. However, despite these and other setbacks on 22 August, a certain number of French counter-attacks carried out on 23 August met with success. In particular, Franchet d'Espèrey's I Corps, on the east, managed to take back positions along the Meuse. On the west, it was troops of XVIII Corps commanded by General Charles Mangin, having just arrived at the front, who pushed back the Germans trying to advance.

In the evening of 23 August, the overall situation of the French Fifth Army thus remained uncertain. Lanrezac learned at this time that Fourth Army, on his right, had experienced serious reversals and was pulling back. On his left, he was anticipating an enveloping manoeuvre by the German First

Army and had no faith in the British Expeditionary Force to oppose it. In the north, he noted that the last Belgian troops were withdrawing from Namur, whose forts had been crushed, one after the other, by Germany's 420-mm mortars. Feeling betrayed by the initiatives of his corps commanders, he no longer trusted their ability to maintain tactical discipline. The isolated successes of the French counter-attacks on 23 August had temporarily loosened the grip of the opposing forces. Without consulting Joffre, Lanrezac then decided in favour of retreat and ordered the entire Fifth Army to pull back to a line stretching from Givet to Maubeuge. His decision sparked anger among some of his own staff officers, exasperated that the Fifth Army was pulling back even though it had not been beaten decisively on the various battlefields. Intellectually, it was an unacceptable choice for officers trained in the cult of the offensive.[107] Lanrezac, who was no ardent follower of that cult, took no notice of their objections.

The withdrawal order issued to the Fifth Army led to an overall retreat by French troops along the entire front, from east to west. In the Ardennes, the French Fourth and Third Armies had already been compelled to return to their starting positions after the bloody setbacks of 22 August. In Alsace and in Lorraine, the French First and Second Armies had also been retreating for two days in response to the German counter-attack launched on 20 August. As for the British Expeditionary Force, it had just taken up position on the Fifth Army's left flank, outside the city of Mons, and the advance guards of the German First Army had begun to attack its positions. The British Expeditionary Force's military capacity was in fact excellent, despite the low opinion held by Lanrezac of its superior officers. In previous encounters, their outstanding rifle skills had enabled British troops in relatively small numbers to completely decimate assault waves of Zulu warriors, Sudanese dervishes, Indian mutineers and Boer commandos. And once again at Mons, the accurate fire laid down by British professional soldiers had pushed back German troops, inflicting heavy losses.[108] But Lanrezac's retreat would force the British, who had only just arrived, to pull back quickly.

At this point, the French armies were thoroughly exhausted. The men had been brutally ripped from their homes or their barracks just three weeks earlier. Ten days before, they had arrived, by rail, at their respective concentration points in north-eastern France. They had then covered huge distances on foot each day, burdened with their heavy packs, under the August sun. Most recently, in the last few hours, most of them had been engaged in fighting of unprecedented violence, which had annihilated many of the units taking part. In particular, these encounters had decimated the ranks of subalterns and non-commissioned officers, always the most exposed to fire. Nevertheless, the French were not entirely beaten back. On the contrary, from one end to the other of the front, a certain number of counter-attacks and momentary successes – at Le Cateau, Guise and Nancy – afforded the French armies a slight respite, which they used to reorganize effectively. At the same time, the tactical choices of the German general staff caused them to depart gradually, both intellectually and materially, from the Schlieffen Plan's guidelines. It was the cumulative effect of this French resilience and these German errors that would make possible the tide-turning battle known as the 'Miracle of the Marne'.

Soldiers on the German side were just as worn out as their French counterparts. The troops on the west, in particular the German First and Second Armies, the largest in number, had covered several hundred kilometres, also on foot, in less than two weeks. Moreover, unlike their adversaries, the German troops in Belgium were operating in fundamentally hostile territory. The German belief, for the most part uncorroborated, that Belgian snipers had them in their sights at every turn kept the troops permanently on their guard, a particularly exhausting stance.[109]

Due to Moltke's personal style, his various army commanders were left considerable room for initiative. Until 20 August, the German army headquarters had remained in Germany, first in Berlin and then in Koblenz, about 300 kilometres from the western portion of the front. It then moved to Luxembourg to be closer to operations, but with a skeleton general staff and a limited communications system. Monitored much less by Moltke than their French counterparts were by Joffre, German army commanders acted independently of each other, for the most part. With the exception of Bülow, who had been given overall responsibility for Kluck's First Army as well as his own by Moltke in mid-August, German army commanders functioned in a nearly autonomous manner.

In addition, the development of operations led Moltke gradually to distance himself from Schlieffen's envelopment strategy, which sought to overtake French forces using a powerful German right wing. A first major divergence was to allow the German Sixth and Seventh Armies, after having beaten back the French offensive in Lorraine on 20 August, to counter-attack and seek to capture Nancy, even to attempt to break through further into French territory by rushing into the Charmes Gap. The German strategy had always been to refrain from directly attacking France's fortifications in the eastern part of the country. Given this latitude to pursue, on French territory, the armies defeated in the Ardennes, this strategy evolved into a quest, by each German army, for the decisive battle and the ultimate breakthrough. In this regard, Moltke was influenced by the optimistic reports he received from his army commanders. All the notifications received at his main headquarters expressed the same conviction. In practical terms, at each engagement, the German troops had remained the masters of the terrain, although not without sustaining heavy losses. At the same time, the French armies had begun a general retreat along the entire length of the front. Considering that the decisive battle was on the verge of being won and that French resistance was breaking down, Moltke decided first of all to remove three corps from his First Army, thus weakening its effective force to the same extent. The first was assigned to attack what remained of the Belgian army, entrenched outside Antwerp. The other two corps were sent urgently to East Prussia. On the Eastern Front, the Russian troops, who had begun their offensive on 14 August as agreed with their French ally, were covering ground more quickly than anticipated.[110] Moltke also decided to assign an army corps to besiege the fort protecting Maubeuge, although it had no real strategic importance and was defended by territorial units, who resisted courageously until 8 September. Lastly, he left another army corps in charge of occupying Brussels and its region. In all, the combined forces of the three armies on the German right wing were reduced from sixteen to eleven corps. The absence of these five corps would have drastic consequences, on the German side, during the Battle of the Marne.

In fact, the French armies did pull back consistently across the front as a whole but, in spite of the exhausted troops, heavy losses sustained and logistical disarray, they retained, if not complete, at least effective fighting capacity. This is the foundation on which the French command would rely to finally halt the German advance.

On the French side, as Joffre had not published or officially circulated his strategic plans, it was a confoundingly simple matter to change them. In four days of fighting, from 20 to 24 August, France clearly lost what would come to be known as the 'Battle of the Frontiers'. The invasion routes into the country from the north were now open. A new strategic plan was therefore necessary. As early as 25 August, Joffre acknowledged the failure of his previous initiatives – although not before making sure to lay blame on those carrying them out, namely the troops under his orders and their commanders. Although he managed to operate outside the control of the war ministry, Joffre had enough political finesse to keep Messimy personally informed of the development of operations, at least in the way in which Joffre himself wanted to present them. Three successive messages sent to Messimy are worth citing here.

The first is the one sent on 20 August, after the initial setbacks in Lorraine:

> The offensive in Lorraine got off to a great start. But this momentum was abruptly cut short by individual and collective failings, which led to a general retreat and cost us very heavy losses. I ordered XV Corps, which had been unable to hold firm under fire, thus scuttling our offensive, to pull back to the rear. I am initiating firm court-martial proceedings.[111]

On 23 August, once the retreat of the dog-tired French forces in the Ardennes had begun, Joffre wrote the following:

> On the whole, the strategic manoeuvre has been completed. It has achieved the desired outcome of putting the bulk of our troops at what should be the enemy's most vulnerable point, thus ensuring our numerical superiority there. The ball is now in the court of those implementing the strategy, who need to make the most of this superiority.[112]

Lastly, on 24 August, not surprisingly, he continued as follows:

> My fears over the previous days about the offensive aptitude of our troops in open terrain were confirmed by yesterday's events.[113]

Joffre's first initiative was to give his approval for a retreat by the French left wing, at the outset to a line extending from Maubeuge to Mézières to Verdun. He later altered the arrangement of his troops by extracting some from the right to create a new Sixth Army, under General Maunoury. It was to take up position on the left of Lanrezac's Fifth Army and the British Expeditionary Force. Joffre and his general staff were trying to build up a force able to attack and vanquish Kluck's First Army, a task that had been beyond the capabilities of Lanrezac and John French until then. In order to move the troops, the army's transport division set a tremendous plan in motion, mobilizing hundreds of trains in the space of just seventy-two hours. Joffre's last step was to attempt to gain the cooperation of French and Lanrezac, who were falling back under the weight of heavy German assaults, but were avoiding communication with GQG and could certainly not be said to be cooperating. On 26 August, too tired to fall back any more, the British troops engaged Kluck's First Army in the Battle of Le Cateau. As at Mons, British soldiers demonstrated their phenomenally effective rifle fire. However, in contrast to the industrial urban landscape of Mons, the arid and flat terrain of the Le Cateau plateau offered very little shelter to those on the defensive. The British infantry, exposed to German artillery, found themselves quickly outmanoeuvred. They would be saved, late in the afternoon, by a charge from Sordet's cavalry corps, one of the last mounted charges carried out on the Western Front.

However, at nightfall in the pouring rain, the British troops attempted to continue their retreat under fire. This day would go down in history as the bloodiest for the British army since Waterloo.[114] Joffre feared that French was becoming disheartened and guided his retreat to the ports along the English Channel to re-embark his troops. He thus sent a liaison officer to Lanrezac to require that he stop his own retreat and counter-attack the German First Army, so as to allow the British troops to withdraw. Lanrezac immediately sent Joffre's liaison officer back to GQG, although not without first having personally lambasted him with a short but stern speech on the incompetence of the French general staff. To bring Lanrezac in line and ensure that he would cover the retreat of the British Expeditionary Force, Joffre thus had to pay a personal visit to the headquarters of a general who was, in principle, his subordinate. After a heated discussion in which Lanrezac tried to convince Joffre of his troops' state of extreme exhaustion, he agreed to attack only if Joffre provided the order in writing. The commander-in-chief, livid with rage, had to sit down that instant at the closest table at hand and write up the order himself.[115]

This engagement demanded by Joffre would be known as the Battle of Guise (or Saint-Quentin for the Germans). On 29 August, the German Second Army, which had just crossed the river Oise, was expecting the French Fifth Army to continue its withdrawal. In fact, the latter interrupted its retreat and three of its army corps vigorously counter-attacked the surprised German troops. Fighting was intense until the following evening, with heavy losses on both sides. Joffre, now entirely distrustful of Lanrezac, even travelled to his headquarters in Laon, remaining there all morning on 30 August to monitor the execution of his orders. Relieved to find that he was finally being obeyed, he returned to Château-Thierry in the late afternoon.[116] In the evening, Joffre's general staff authorized the Fifth Army to retire and continue its withdrawal. The thirty-six-hour interruption in the German advance, combined with the successes of Foch's XX Corps in Lorraine, outside Nancy and in the Charmes Gap, would permit the British and the other French armies to continue their withdrawal without struggling under enemy fire. From 30 August, the Germans were unable to massively attack French troops until they met up with them again, six days later, at the start of the Battle of the Marne.

In the interim, Kluck was clearly interested in pursuing his quest for the decisive battle that he thought was taking shape earlier than anticipated, on the left of his own army. As the French forces had been driven back at Guise, Bülow burst forth with triumphant notifications sent to the German general staff and the other army commanders. Even if some on the German side noted the considerable extent of their own losses as well as their inability to lead a rapid pursuit after the fighting on 30 August, many believed that the war was on the verge of being won. The decision taken by Kluck to change the direction of his army's advance from south-west to south-east, which he believed would allow him to beat back the French troops definitively, would result in a series of fatal consequences for the German offensive in 1914.

First of all, it put the final nail in the coffin of the Schlieffen Plan to envelop the French forces. Secondly, Kluck allowed the French general staff time to build up a sizeable Sixth Army on its west. By changing direction and suspending the drive towards Paris, he freed the troops intended to ensure the capital's defence, who were thus able to take part in the counter-offensive.[117] Lastly, he opened the flank of his army to attack by the freshly constituted Sixth Army and its energized troops. The ensuing battle east of Paris, now known as the Battle of the Marne, would mark the definitive end of the German battle plan in the west.

Today, many are familiar with this First Battle of the Marne. Conversely, the details of the extraordinarily violent engagements having preceded it are little known. From a strategic standpoint, the Battle of the Marne cannot blot out the disastrous consequences of the failures during the Battle of the Frontiers. First of all, the vast territory abandoned during the retreat would allow the German armies to select favourable positions, such as ridges, when falling back along the entire front, from Mulhouse to Ypres. Virtually the entire war on the Western Front would thus be waged on a narrow strip of French soil.[118] Considerable human, agricultural, mining and industrial resources were relinquished to the enemy and were thus no longer available for the war effort. Above all, both sides gradually built up an elaborate network of defensive trenches, thus marking the end of the war of movement. A new way of waging war was emerging, placing emphasis on artillery, communications, camouflage, and so on. However, French military commanders would only adapt very slowly to the new conditions, whereas the Germans would prove more effective at reaping lessons from successive encounters. Without a doubt, the fact that Joffre remained at the helm until 1916 slowed down, or prevented, any analysis of French military shortcomings in 1914 as well as any reflections on the weaknesses of his doctrine and organization or the errors committed during the first month of the war. Furthermore, the offensives led under Joffre's orders (Artois, Champagne) all sought to engineer a return to the war of movement as it had been described in Plan XVII. These offensives would make 1915 the bloodiest year of the war for the French, without achieving any tactical benefit whatsoever.

CHAPTER 8

CIVILIANS IN GERMAN CROSS HAIRS

During the first weeks of the war, a very large number of civilians were killed in Belgian battle zones and, to a lesser extent, in those in north-eastern France.

Most of these civilian casualties did not result from collateral damage (errant bullets, shelling, spreading of fires, and so on), even when military operations took place in densely populated areas. In fact, a sizeable majority of the civilians who died in the first weeks of the war were deliberately killed by German troops. Most of these deaths occurred in connection with fighting on the front lines, or in close proximity to this fighting, in either time or space. A comparatively small number of civilians were killed in the course of incidents behind the front lines, most often at night, far from the battles. Lastly, other civilians were purely and simply executed outside battle periods and zones, occasionally following a summary judgement.

In their seminal work on this subject, John Horne and Alan Kramer enumerate a total of 6,427 civilians deliberately killed by the Germans in Belgium and France, in the course of about 500 incidents.[119] These civilian deaths were distributed geographically across the entire theatre of operations and involved, to varying extents, almost all of the units taking part in the offensive in the west. However, the bloodiest episodes took place during the third week of the war, in particular at Tamines on 22 August (383 killed), at Dinant on 23 August (687 killed) and at Leuven on 25 August (248 killed). As for the French troops, the deadliest twenty-four-hour period of the entire war for civilians was between 22 and 23 August, with a total of 2,000 civilians killed, including 123 in France. These deaths were the result of thirty-two separate events across all battle zones, from the Belgian province of Brabant in the west to the French *département* of Meurthe-et-Moselle in the east.

Horne and Kramer provide a wealth of statistics. In addition to civilians killed, they also give an account of hostages used as human shields during battles and deportations of civilians, as well as the destruction of civilian buildings, most notably the fire laying waste to the university library in Leuven. On the other hand, they do not take into account rapes committed by soldiers, which were nonetheless frequent.[120] The German authorities, for their part, did not deny the executions, especially since they had been public and were intended to serve as examples and as a means of intimidation. In most cases, the authorities spoke of aggressive attacks by *francs-tireurs* against German troops to justify the legitimacy of these actions.

THE FRANCO-PRUSSIAN WAR AND THE LEGEND OF THE *FRANCS-TIREURS*

Until the surrender by the Second Empire's armies at Sedan in early September 1870, then at Metz in late October, this conflict between France and Germany had opposed two 'traditional' armies. But after the republican uprising on 4 September in Paris, irregular units of volunteer civilians were formed here and there, wearing a motley collection of makeshift uniforms and equipped to varying degrees. These groups called themselves *francs-tireurs* (literally 'free shooters') or *corps francs* ('free corps'), two terms that had been coined in 1792 to designate units of partisans, non-professional volunteers coming to the aid of the regular army to defend the nation's borders. Furthermore, in November 1870, the fledgling Third Republic invoked the memory of the 1793 *levée en masse* (when all of the able-bodied were summoned to defend the country), by specifically calling for the support of the entire population. A republican army was formed, bringing together active troops, mobile national guard units, units of *francs-tireurs* as well as units of foreign volunteers, such as that led by Garibaldi. In all, there were 300 units of *francs-tireurs*, numbering more than 57,000 men.

The Prussian reaction to this *levée en masse* and the use of volunteer partisans was a mix of rage and consternation. In the first place, the Prussians had the feeling that they had already won the war with the surrender of the Imperial armies. The continuation of the conflict, now against a relatively amorphous enemy, was experienced not merely as an unpleasant surprise, but more precisely as a form of treachery or 'betrayal'. Since Napoleon III's army had been conquered on the battlefield, would it not be more appropriate for France to accept defeat? Moreover, the concept of a mass appeal was shocking to an aristocratic army like that of the Prussians, proud of its elite standing, its professionalism, and ardently opposed to arming the general population. Such an idea reminded the Prussians of Germany's internal upheavals in 1848, which its army had helped repress. In addition, this concept raised a complex set of military challenges, as the Prussian army was conceived to combat an enemy similar in composition to itself, grouped into recognizable and organized units, which it aimed to annihilate in a single decisive battle. Fighting against myriad small groups distributed across a vast territory, not always easy to distinguish from civilians, presented numerous difficulties. At this time, there was still a clear separation between civilians and soldiers. Not only did a civilian not resemble a soldier, but there was little opportunity for contact between them, except when the former was watching the latter in a parade. Civilians had no place either on the battlefield or in the surrounding area. Any civilian presence was regarded with suspicion, since the individual might be there to retrieve valuable items from cadavers or, worse yet, spy on the troops for the enemy. On top of this, in order for the Prussians to transition from an army engaged in a campaign to an occupying force facing a popular insurrection, they needed troops in far greater numbers, particularly to protect depots and supply routes.

Forced to prolong the war, the Prussians thus granted the legal status of combatant to the Republic's regular armies but refused this status to partisans, considered as unlawful or 'treacherous' combatants. For example, the latter would not be offered the protection granted to prisoners of war. Consequently, Moltke, the chief of the general staff, interested in protecting transit routes and particularly the railways, ordered reprisals against any villages in proximity to which incidents creating disruptions in rail transport would occur:

> In cases of frequent disturbance the mayor or other local notables were to be placed as hostages on the locomotives. Where civilians actively resisted, contributions were to be exacted from the community, and in the case of large-scale participation the entire village was to be destroyed.[121]

For the German military, the adequate response to civilian involvement in warfare was thus a form of terror by way of reprisals. On this point, Horne and Kramer quote a letter written by Moltke in late October 1870, in which he offers a subtle and carefully considered analysis of the dangers of a war expanded in scope to include entire populations, in comparison with a war conducted by armies:

The [republican] government is still trying [...] to rouse the unfortunate population of the provinces to a new resistance, which will entail the destruction of whole towns if it is to be put down. Then, too, the nagging of the *francs-tireurs* will need to be answered by bloody reprisals, and the character of the war will become ever more vindictive. It is bad enough that armies sometimes have to butcher one another; there is no necessity for setting whole nations against each other – that is not progress, but rather a return to barbarism.[122]

In line with Prussian doctrine, victory should result from a single decisive and extremely violent battle. If an entire population were to go up against the German forces and chose to take part in the fighting, it would lay itself open to a military kind of violence, but on a broader scale.

From 1871 to 1914, German diplomats and military commanders had continued to debate the question of the behaviour to be adopted in the face of popular insurrections in general, and irregular combatants in particular. The 1899 and 1907 Hague Conventions, which aimed specifically at reducing the horrors of warfare, sought to define a combatant status that would be acceptable for all the major powers. In drafting this definition, the Western powers (France, Great Britain, Holland and Belgium) stood in opposition to the Continental empires (Russia, Germany). The former group managed to ensure that the *levée en masse*, as a complement to a professional army, would be considered a legitimate recourse. Russia and Germany successfully established that militias and volunteer corps would need, in order to be protected by the agreement, to be placed under the leadership of a responsible commander, wear fixed distinctive signs and carry arms openly. Like many diplomatic compromises, this one paved the way for differences in interpretation that would have fatal consequences in the field.

Within the German army, the question of *francs-tireurs* had continued to serve as grist for conversations among officers and troops. The risk of having to face irregular troops in a conflict in the west was discussed at length, usually reaching the conclusion that *francs-tireurs* needed to be handled with extreme severity. The desired objective was to obtain, through terror, the complete submission of the headstrong population. Whereas in France the subject did not seem to be a matter of great concern, it preoccupied generations nearly to obsession in Germany, even beyond military circles. Popular novels and other fiction serialized in the press frequently referred to *francs-tireurs*, playing up a variety of tortures and brutalities (eyes gouged out, ears and noses cut off, beheadings, and so on) supposedly inflicted during the Franco-Prussian War on German soldiers treacherously attacked by armed civilians. The German military's views on the manner in which it would behave in response to such hostilities in France or Belgium are reflected in its internal publications. In 1906, it thus issued a French-conversation manual for the use of its officers. It is instructive to quote two of its 'useful phrases' (given in French in the manual): '*Francs-tireurs* are outlaws and are to be shot when they are captured' and 'Since several assassinations have been committed by *francs-tireurs* hidden in the nearby woods, I order as follows: "Every individual encountered within the woods will be considered a *franc-tireur* and treated accordingly."'[123]

GERMAN ARMED FORCES AND THE COLONIES (1900-14)

Although, the potential behaviour of the German army towards civilians in Europe remained a matter of supposition, or even fantasy, until 1914, its practices in other places in the early twentieth century had been abundantly documented. German forces were active in China in 1900–1901 in the aftermath of the Boxer Rebellion, in German East Africa (Tanganyika) in 1902, and in German South West Africa (annihilation of the Herero in present-day Namibia) in 1904. On these occasions, the application of the German military doctrine known as

Vernichtungskrieg ('extermination war') began to slip from the military into the civilian realm.[124]

THE BOXER REBELLION

At the turn of the twentieth century, a popular uprising by the Boxers[125] broke out in China, who were protesting as much against Manchu rule, centred in Beijing, as against the growing political, economic and intellectual influence in the country of the great Western powers and Japan. Little by little, the movement became a full-fledged rebellion, targeting all foreigners, particularly diplomats and Christian missionaries. Missionaries, priests and nuns, often German natives as it happened, were thus massacred along with thousands of Chinese who had converted to Catholicism. The Manchu rulers, who were trying to co-opt the movement and use it against Westerners, allowed the protesters to organize, and even lent support to coordinate troops of Boxers in Beijing. These lay siege to the foreign embassies of the Legation Quarter, where many other Westerners also lived. The assassination, on 20 June 1900, of the German diplomat Baron von Ketteler marked the beginning of the offensive in this district, transforming embassies into entrenched camps, defended by small groups of soldiers along with armed Western civilians. This siege would last for fifty-five days, before the rebellion was crushed by an international force of some 20,000 troops under the command of the British general Sir Alfred Gaselee. About half of these soldiers were Japanese, while the remainder were comprised of British, American, German, French, Austro-Hungarian, Italian and Russian contingents. Gaselee's troops reached the outskirts of Beijing on 14 August, where they confronted and defeated the Boxers in three successive battles. Once their military might was shattered, the Manchu government turned against the rebels and those who had played leading parts in the movement were executed, or forced into exile. Westerners and the Japanese then expanded their local military presence to gain greater influence with the Chinese government and negotiate new treaties.

On 27 July 1900, it was in the following terms that Kaiser Wilhelm II addressed the troops about to depart to join the German contingent to suppress the Boxer Rebellion:

Should you encounter the enemy, he will be defeated! No quarter will be given! Prisoners will not be taken! Whoever falls into your hands is forfeited. Just as a thousand years ago the Huns under their King Attila made a name for themselves [...] may the name German be affirmed by you in such a way in China that no Chinese will ever again dare to look cross-eyed at a German.[126]

Field Marshal Alfred von Waldersee, assisted by Lieutenant General Lothar von Trotha, who had shown his skills in the brutal subjugation of the indigenous people in Tanganyika, was then given command of a German expeditionary corps, numbering about 18,000 men. In October 1900, by which time the Boxer Rebellion had already been routed, the German army launched a large-scale campaign of reprisals against Chinese civilians. This campaign lasted until the autumn of 1901 and the signing of a peace treaty between China, the seven Western powers and Japan on 7 September. In the interim, dozens of punitive expeditions had been launched from Beijing into the countryside intended to bring to a definitive end all Boxer resistance; more than half of these expeditions were by German units, whose use of indiscriminate and extreme violence against the civilian population, even children, women and the elderly, has been widely recognized, a rampage that included rape and massive destruction of property. The death toll, which is difficult to determine accurately, may have numbered in the tens of thousands.

The Herero genocide

In the 1880s, Germany began to display increasing interest in closing the gap with its French and especially British rivals in the formation of a colonial empire, as acquiring colonies was deemed necessary for the development of its economy and in order to maintain its stature as a great power. By this time, Africa was the only one of the world's continents that still offered opportunities for conquest. Convened by the German chancellor, Otto von Bismarck, a meeting of European colonial powers was held from November 1884 to February 1885, now known as the Berlin Conference, which resulted in an agreement carving up the African continent. In addition to the official recognition of existing possessions and spheres of influence in Africa, this treaty also stipulated rules for future claims to territories not yet colonized by Europeans, stating that any new occupation had to be formally notified to the other signatory powers. Following in the footsteps of its missionaries, merchants, soldiers and settlers, Germany was thus able to expand successfully its presence in southeast Africa (Tanganyika, Rwanda, which became German East Africa), in equatorial Africa (Togo, Cameroon) and in South West Africa, which had become a German protectorate in 1884.

In contrast to the other colonies, South West Africa was considered to offer great potential for settlements. Serving as the protectorate's governor general from 1885 to 1890, Heinrich Göring, father of the future Nazi official, led a campaign to encourage immigration by German farmers and ranchers, in conjunction with land-alienation policies. This land belonged to three distinct ethnic groups: the Herero, the Nama and the Ovambo. In January 1904, the first of these, with a population of about 80,000, rose up against German rule, with several early successes. In particular, they managed to occupy a German fort, where they slaughtered male settlers and garrison soldiers (but spared women, children and missionaries).

On 11 June 1904, General von Trotha, selected on the basis of his 'successes' in Tanganyika and China, arrived in South West Africa with an expeditionary force, having been vested with full powers to deal with this uprising. In August, he encircled the insurgents in the Waterberg area, where they had gathered with their families and herds. German military superiority led to a massacre and a Herero defeat. The survivors fled into the Kalahari Desert. Trotha cordoned off escape routes with a 250-kilometre-long chain of military outposts, ordering his soldiers to poison all the waterholes. Many Herero died a slow death in the desert from thirst and starvation. On 2 October, Trotha issued an official extermination order (*Vernichtungsbefehl*) whose tone was terse and matter-of-fact: 'Within the German borders every Herero, with or without a gun, with or without cattle, will be shot.'[127] At the urging of Chancellor von Bülow, an order countermanding Trotha's proclamation was ratified by the Emperor on 8 December 1904, after which captured Herero were placed in what were officially described as concentration camps (*Konzentrationslager*) and put to work as forced labourers.[128] The invention of this concept is often attributed to the Spanish, who responded in 1896 to the growing insurrection in Cuba by instituting a *reconcentrado* (reconcentration) system, but this involved more precisely the separation of insurgents from the civilian population by moving the latter to fortified towns.[129] These fortified towns were the forerunners of the concentration camps used by the British in South Africa during the Boer War (1899–1902) to confine Boer non-combatants.

Although both the Spanish and British systems subjected inhabitants to miserable living conditions, leaving them prey to disease and thus resulting in thousands of deaths, German concentration camps in South West Africa were different from their predecessors in two important ways. The rations given to Herero prisoners were heavily restricted, and they were subjected to various kinds of ill treatment, over and above their use as a source of slave labour (for building railways, unloading cargo from ships and so on).[130] To this end, several major private German companies ran their own camps.[131] This was also the first time that prisoners would be branded on their forearms, here with the letters 'GH', standing for *gefangene Herero* (captured Herero).

In these camps, which rapidly became work camps and not only internment camps, the mortality rate rose to about 50 per cent. Moreover, inspired by the German eugenics movement that had arisen during the Wilhelmine period, medical experiments were carried out on the cadavers of prisoners, notably by Dr Eugen Fischer.[132] News of these extreme measures would eventually reach Germany. From the floor of the Reichstag, the Social Democratic leader August Bebel chastised the government, exclaiming that 'any butcher's boy would have waged war just as well as Herr von Trotha!'[133] Protestant missionaries also expressed their indignation and even some colonial settlers, concerned that their entire potential workforce was being wiped out, voiced their opposition to the methods employed. In November 1905, again at the urging of Chancellor von Bülow, Wilhelm II reluctantly relieved General von Trotha of his command.

By 1911, when an official census was carried out, there were only 15,130 Herero left in German South West Africa, thus about 20 per cent of their population according to missionary accounts in 1904.

The entry of German troops into Belgium

From their obsession with *francs-tireurs* as a legacy of the Franco-Prussian War to their more recent history of colonial violence, it seems indisputable that the German military entered the First World War in an extremely repressive stance vis-à-vis the civilian populations of enemy countries. Violent acts against civilians thus began almost immediately once the German troops entered Belgium on 4 August, under the influence of several factors.

VISIONS OF FRANCS-TIREURS

Since 1871, the German army had thus been stoking its fear of having to contend with armed civilians on the Western Front. Internal debates veered between the alarming catalogue of atrocities likely to be inflicted on German soldiers by civilians and plans for reprisals in response. Put simply, the German army had been so convinced, and for so long, that their men would come up against *francs-tireurs* that, once the war began, they became certain that they were encountering quite a few of them. Field records of military units, stories appearing in the German press of course, but also the private correspondence of combatants, from the rank and file to superior officers, were filled from the very first day with reports of shooting and attacks committed by Belgian civilians against German troops. Most of these are indirect accounts, but some refer to incidents that the writers themselves claim to have witnessed. But none of these occurrences was ever corroborated by an independent inquiry, either during the war or once the conflict had ended. In order to explain what they call the 'collective delusion' propagating the fear of *francs-tireurs*, Horne and Kramer draw on studies of social psychology as well as history.

They refer in particular to Georges Lefebvre's seminal work on the 'Great Fear' of 1789.[134] In the summer of that year, the belief in the imminent invasion of France by bands of brigands with ties to the aristocracy spread like wildfire throughout the country. This fear, conjured up by the population in the form of an apocalyptic vision, had led to the (very real) pillage and destruction of countless castles and noble homes, together with many acts of violence and extortion against aristocrats and their families. For this historian of the French Revolution, what distinguishes 'fear' is the utter conviction that the illusory event is actually occurring: 'When a gathering, an army or an entire population fully expects an enemy to arrive, it becomes highly unlikely for them not to catch sight of this enemy.'[135]

SURPRISING RESISTANCE BY THE BELGIAN ARMY

One of the intended advantages of the Schlieffen Plan, apart from circumventing the French fortifications, was to ensure that German forces would initially come up against an enemy known to be weak. In early August 1914, the Belgian army consisted of about 150,000 men, including members of local civilian militias, following a practice that dated back to the Middle Ages. A law enacting universal male conscription had been passed in 1913, but its provisions had yet to completely enter into force. Known collectively as the Garde Civique, local militias throughout the country supplemented Belgium's small standing army. The Germans calculated that the latter would not be likely to offer any serious resistance, which allowed them to envisage a quick sweep through Belgium, as an essential prerequisite to ensure the success of their plan. Germany also hoped that its neighbour, in the interests of avoiding losses and devastation, would not put up any opposition to its advance. On 4 August, at the moment when its troops were crossing the border along a forty-kilometre front stretching from Aachen to Montmédy, Germany thus officially requested free passage for its troops across Belgian territory to counter a French attack characterized as 'imminent'. However, on 5 August, Belgium declared that it was at war with Germany as a result of this invasion.

General Otto von Emmich, the commander of the special

task force assigned to take Liège, had issued a declaration in which he stated that the Belgians would not be considered enemies. Emmich said that the Germans were only interested in obtaining free passage, although he warned that they would respond harshly in the event of sabotage. But from the entry by the Germans into Belgium on 4 August, the fierce resistance of the Belgian troops, not to mention the strength of the Liège fort system, surprised the German army, which sustained heavy losses. Under fire, the Germans were forced to abandon certain districts of Liège. This unanticipated initial shock, combined with the assumption that *francs-tireurs* were hiding behind every corner, would have serious consequences for the behaviour of German troops. Horne and Kramer sum up the state of mind of these soldiers and officers as follows: 'The German troops anticipated civilian resistance from the start and considered this to be wholly against the laws of war and proper military conduct. Many felt national self-defence by the Belgian army to be unjustified.'[136] Whether civilian or military, Belgian resistance was thus perceived by the Germans as futile, immoral and probably unlawful. It was therefore met with immediate and severe reprisals.

THE FOG OF MODERN WAR

Confrontations between Belgian and German soldiers did not take place on a traditional battlefield. From the first day, nearly a million troops on the German side were crossing into Belgium through a corridor forty kilometres wide, thus offering the Belgians a multitude of targets. In addition, this area was at the time, and remains, one of the most urbanized and densely populated regions in the world. Across the area, factories, warehouses and commercial buildings were intermingled with individual homes, schools and churches, giving defenders plenty of places to use for protection or hide from attackers. Moreover, modern individual weapons, equipped with high-velocity ammunition, could be used to fire accurately more than a kilometre from a target, especially if the shooter had a place to rest his weapon, such as a window ledge. A German soldier moving through the districts of Liège, Namur, Dinant or Leuven would be apt to be hit from anywhere by enemy fire that he would be unable to see and whose precise origin it would thus be very difficult to determine. As a matter of course, it was concluded that this invisible and faceless enemy could only be a *franc-tireur*. He was potentially any male individual who might cross the soldier's path and, from that moment, would become a legitimate target for justified reprisals. These reprisals even seem to have been encouraged in an increasingly conscious manner by German superior officers, with the mounting success of the Belgian resistance at slowing the invader's advance threatening to derail the very exacting schedule of the Schlieffen Plan.

Nervousness, Darkness, Drunkenness

Several years into the war, the battle-weary soldiers facing each other from their respective trenches would develop a fine ability to interpret each sound, each detonation. In an instant, they would be able to identify the weapon used, its calibre, the location of the shooter, the projectile's probable trajectory and the danger posed. But in August 1914, the soldiers who had just entered Belgium were far from having acquired such knowledge. Each explosion took them by surprise and was likely to trigger a chaos of shooting, with the Germans often catching each other in the crossfire. Darkness was an additional factor when a number of different units were moving through very unfamiliar countryside. Another aggravating factor, of course, was the massive consumption of alcohol in all forms (beer, wine and spirits), depending on what could be found at a given site as an antidote to the forced march under the blazing heat. Moreover, rumours were rife that the Belgians had poisoned the wells or, worse, the water that some of them offered to soldiers from the side of the road. In short, the constrained proximity of exhausted, excited, frightened and often intoxicated troops facing a large population viewed as hostile created a dangerous situation for these civilians.

Burgomasters and Parish Priests as Scapegoats

Whether the incidents involved simple threats or actual reprisals perpetrated against the civilian population, two groups were singled out in particular by German troops. Burgomasters, the chief magistrates of Belgian towns, roughly equivalent to English mayors, were quite logically the first targets. They were the ones able to take the initiative to make declarations to the local population, in order to communicate instructions and threats on behalf of the Germans. In general, they were the first hostages to be taken, often along with their families, a role they frequently shared with the local parish priests.

As a matter of fact, parish priests, monks and nuns were subjected to particularly brutal treatment, because German troops perceived the Belgian population as completely controlled by the Catholic Church. The Germans presumed that resistance activities were being coordinated, even initiated, by the clergy, considered the only real local authority. Furthermore, the church in each village was seen as a source of danger, particularly its bell tower, based on the notion that signals would be sent from there to the Belgian or French troops in the area, to alert them about German troop movements. Frequently, the invaders were convinced that they were being fired upon from bell towers, going so far as to assume that machine guns were installed in these belfries. During this initial phase of the war, the German forces were still organized on the basis of recruitment at the regional level. The German First, Second and Third Armies entering into Belgium consisted for the most part of Prussian or Saxon soldiers, who were therefore Lutherans. This denominational distinction is not without significance, for two reasons. Germany had only recently emerged from the *Kulturkampf*, the 'struggle for civilization' between the state and liberals, on the one hand, and the Catholic Church on the other, which was brought to an end with the official separation of church and state. In addition, the memory of the wars of religion that had ravaged the country for two centuries was still vivid. The destruction of the famed Leuven university library was thus explicitly linked to its status as a symbol of Catholic education in the country. Churches were frequently pillaged, raids during which many ritual objects were destroyed, while soldiers took to strutting about wearing liturgical ornaments. When not razed to the ground, places of worship were often sullied, the troops forcing the clergymen to parade before them to be spat upon, poked and jabbed, before being thrashed within an inch of their lives or simply executed. It is striking to note the extent to which clergymen, much more than other civilians, were frequently beaten, humiliated and even tortured before being killed.

THE MASSACRES AT TAMINES ON 22 AUGUST[137]

After Dinant, where more than 670 Belgian civilians were killed on 23 August, it was in Tamines, a small suburb of Charleroi, that the war's second-largest massacre of Belgian civilians was committed, on 22 August. On the previous day, the German Second Army, which had just taken Namur and was moving towards Charleroi, had begun to be attacked by units of Lanrezac's Fifth Army. Along with several units of the Belgian Garde Civique, the French soldiers had tried to prevent the advance of the German troops, focusing in particular on keeping them from crossing the Sambre. Well entrenched, the French troops had only fallen back slowly and had inflicted severe casualties on the attackers (leaving about 600 dead on 21 August). Despite their frequent use of Belgian civilians encountered along the way as human shields, the Germans only gained control of the bridges at around noon on 22 August.

In the meantime, the civilian population of Tamines had sought refuge in the church to escape the fighting and fires, but also to avoid being taken as hostages. At about 7 p.m., several hours after the fighting with the French troops had ended, the male civilians were ordered out of the church. Six hundred of them were led, in rows four abreast, to the town's main square, on the banks of the Sambre. They found themselves facing a firing squad consisting of seventy soldiers in five rows, the first of which was kneeling in the front. A German officer stepped forward, announcing to the civilians that because they had fired on German soldiers, they would be executed. A whistle was heard and a first salvo was unleashed. All the hostages sank to the ground; those in the first rows had been either killed or wounded, but at the rear many were still unscathed. The Germans shouted at them to stand up and many complied. The squad fired their second salvo. Despite repeated commands from the German officers, no one stood up this time. The squad then tried to direct their fire towards the prostrate civilians, who were either dead, wounded or unharmed. But many of the rounds ricocheted on the ground, placing the Germans nearby in grave danger. So the soldiers stopped firing to move forward, charging at the bodies with their bayonets or beating them with their rifle butts or cudgels. The massacre lasted for nearly an hour. Around 9 p.m., the executioners withdrew from the scene, but not without leaving sentinels behind to prevent the still unscathed – some were hidden among the cadavers – and the wounded from escaping. The sentinels stayed the entire night to keep watch, but some of the survivors took advantage of the darkness to flee by slipping into the river.

On the morning of 23 August, at about 9 a.m., the Germans stormed the church to draw out the women and children who had remained within, whom they assembled along with the men arrested in town the previous evening. Two columns were formed, one with the men, the other with the women and children. Again in rows four abreast, they were led to the main square, which was strewn with cadavers that were beginning to swell under the August sun, other townspeople in the throes of death, and the wounded. Amid the bodies, a few haggard survivors were thus joined by the rest of the town's population. Everyone had to remain standing in the sun among the cadavers, ankle-deep in blood and guts. Early in the afternoon, the men were ordered to dig a pit in a nearby garden. The cadavers were moved and then piled into the pit in several rows before being covered with soil. At 5 p.m., the troops brought together the survivors, who were then led, still in rows four abreast, to the woods north of the town. Once they had arrived at the next village (Velaine), an officer forced the men to shout *'Vive l'Allemagne!'* before adding, 'Now you are free, you may go where you will... But you cannot come home to Tamines before the end of the war.' The village was burned. The official human toll was 423 dead: 315 executed in the square, forty drowned, thirty-one killed elsewhere in the town, thirteen killed in the fires and twenty-four deceased from their wounds.

In the introduction to his classic work on the process of brutalization undergone by European civilization in the aftermath of the First World War as a result of what he terms, with initial capitals for emphasis, the 'Myth of the War Experience', George L. Mosse asks the following question: 'Did the Myth of the War Experience entail a process of brutalization and indifference to individual human life which has perpetuated itself in still greater mass violence in our own time?'[138] But in the very next sentence, he points out that 'the foundations of the Myth of the War Experience were put down long before the First World War'.[139] It certainly seems that the pillars in question were deeply rooted in the military culture of Wilhelmine Germany.

CHAPTER 9

WHY SO MANY DEAD?

The first reason for the exceptionally high number of deaths on 22 August 1914 is that never before had so many men been led into battle at the same time. Three weeks after the start of the war, most of the 1.5 million men mobilized on either side of the Western Front had arrived at their concentration points and were marching towards each other. From the border with Switzerland, where the troops of the new Army of Alsace, under the command of General Pau, had retaken Mulhouse, to the central Belgian city of Mons, where the British Expeditionary Force had just taken up position, fifteen French, British, Belgian and German armies were already fighting each other or would be doing so before the end of the day. The proven capacity of France and Germany to raise, equip and move massive armies was reflected, in the course of the battles, by losses proportional to the number of troops committed. Not all of the soldiers in each army would necessarily see action on 22 August, but a majority of them would in fact find themselves in combat. For the French side, this undoubtedly meant that between 400,000 and 600,000 men were exposed to enemy fire. By comparison, a century earlier, the Battle of Waterloo had opposed two coalition armies that brought together nearly 70,000 men each, with 6,800 killed on the French side.

The second reason lies in the abnormally high number of those injured in battle who succumbed to their wounds. Over the entire duration of the First World War, the ratio of killed to wounded on the French side was about one to three or four. But on 22 August, it was very likely lower than two wounded for every man killed. The macabre accounting of military deaths is a complex affair. Casualties, in military usage, correspond to the number of soldiers who are not at roll call in their respective units the next morning. This group includes those who are killed in action, die afterwards of wounds received in action, are wounded and survive but are unable to return to the fighting, or are known to have been taken prisoner by the enemy, as well as a category understood to be 'missing in action', whose fate is uncertain. Those initially considered to be missing may very well have been killed or wounded, although information on where this happened may not be available. They may also have escaped notice when turning themselves over to the enemy. Or they may have fled, whether or not their aim was desertion. Finally, they may have been either able-bodied or incapacitated after the battle, but temporarily unable to rejoin their units. Over time, many of those listed as missing in action end up being moved to another category.[140] The existence of soldiers who eventually succumb to wounds received in battle after a certain period of time engenders an additional difficulty in determining the number of people whose deaths may be attributed to a given day's fighting.

The ratio of three wounded for every man killed reflects the improved performance, over the duration of the war, of a health system that made great strides between 1914 and 1918.[141] These advances were of several types. First of all, medical, because surgery for the treatment of all types of wounds saw astounding progress, thanks to the accumulation of vast experience in this area. From an organizational standpoint, too, the French medical services gradually became more efficient, in relation both to the retrieval of wounded from the battlefield and the implementation of an entire chain of care (including triage, first used as a diagnostic method on a large scale by the French during this war). Lastly, since the Western Front barely moved over a long period, a particularly effective network of medical units was able to be established, at a number of key points along the relatively stable front.

But none of this existed in August 1914. The French military medical service would only be officially created in 1915. During the mobilization, physicians, very often civilians, were attached to the troops on campaign: they had virtually no experience in the treatment of war wounds. Additionally, as 22 August 1914 was a day in the thick of the war of movement, the French troops hardly had time to set up medical units behind battle lines. Furthermore, in most cases the French left battlefields in the hands of the Germans once the fighting was over, thus abandoning a large number of their wounded, who were not able to withdraw on their own, to the enemy's mercy.

Precisely on this score, the enemy seems to have often come up short, and this lack of compassion is without a doubt a third reason for the high number of deaths. Even taking into account the tendency to paint the opponent's actions in harsh colours, far too many accounts by witnesses or survivors mention cases of wounded having been finished off by the Germans on battlefields that evening for them to be ignored. We must thus picture the German troops scouring the battlefields entirely under their control at the end of the day, on the lookout for abandoned weapons as well as dead and wounded from both sides. The German system for providing assistance to the wounded was also inadequately organized, and just as stretched in its capacity to handle the wounded as its French equivalent. The German soldiers were already physically and mentally drained by the day's fighting. At dawn the following morning, most would have fully expected to continue their punishing advance of the previous days and, very likely, to see fighting again in a matter of hours. This type of situation would hardly encourage them to come to the aid of enemy wounded encountered on the battlefield.[142] Hence they were, at best, indifferent towards those likely to succumb to their wounds and, at worst, tempted to deliver, whether out of spite or fatigue, the fatal blow by bayonet or rifle fire. All of these elements combined to increase further the number of French soldiers killed on this day.

The greater density of firepower, due to the accelerated pace of progress in the design and production of weapons, was also a fundamental factor contributing to the high mortality rate during the first weeks of the war. Compared to the Napoleonic Wars, which at the time remained the point of reference for French military culture, this was a sweeping change. The deadlier effectiveness of firepower surprised the general staff and the officers, but also the rank and file, who would require some time to acquire the habits necessary to protect exposed personnel and, first and foremost, the ability to seek cover continually, and eventually to build trenches. To make matters worse, this increase in firepower density embraced several dimensions. In the first place, it had to do with the rise in the number of combatants and the extensive complement of equipment available: each unit had more guns than in the past, including both artillery pieces and new weapons, such as machine guns. Secondly, rifles, machine guns and artillery all offered a higher rate of fire, making massed infantry charges a suicidal tactic. The effective range of lethal fire had also increased, especially when guns were operated by certain soldiers (British and German, in particular) who had benefited from extensive training with an emphasis on accuracy.[143] These factors combined with the deadlier impact of artillery shells, due as much to their enhanced blast effect as to the sheer numerical expansion of burning-hot metallic fragments dispersed at high speeds.[144] Finally, it is important to mention the more destructive impact of individual projectiles, resulting in large, gaping wounds that were increasingly difficult to treat due to cavitation and the shock waves generated inside the body, together with the disintegration of the bullet itself.

In this context, the spectacular infantry charges during the first days of the war, bayonets at the ready, caused French troops to sustain additional heavy losses. These charges are frequently put forward as the main, if not exclusive, factor to be blamed for the exceptionally high number of French soldiers killed in the early days of the war. However, some military historians, especially those looking at events from the German perspective, find this explanation a bit too facile. For example, Terence Zuber concludes that this type of charge was in fact seldom used and that its presence in documents of the period served for French military officials as a 'presentable' excuse to explain their failures during the Battle of the Frontiers.[145] For this author, the practical application of the all-out attack doctrine was above all a misrepresentation put forward to conceal the German military's obvious tactical superiority at the start of the war. In Zuber's view, the German armed forces were simply better trained, organized and supervised in 1914 than those of any other country in the world, and especially the French, a superiority subsequently demonstrated at each of the engagements on 22 August. This argument is not without merit, even though the French infantry assuredly charged, with bayonets fixed, at a number of sites that day, particularly in the Ardennes, with deadly consequences for the attackers. Indeed, this thesis underscores the French army's remarkable adaptive and transformative capacity beginning in 1914, making all the more astonishing its ability to push back, from September, an adversary effectively superior on so many levels. In a way, the Battle of the Marne was the French army's 'Napoleonic opportunity' in 1914 – a success made possible in part through improvisation, even canny resourcefulness (the taxis of the Marne), which put a wrench in the works of the German military machine.

Along the same lines, it has often been said that the uniform worn by French infantry in August 1914 was a considerable handicap, providing another explanation for the heavy French losses. It is thought that the famous bright-red trousers, in particular, would have made the foot soldiers a devastatingly easy target. But when an infantry charges an enemy having taken cover, especially over an open field in broad daylight, it is not certain what difference, if any, the colour of the men's trousers makes. Would the losses have been significantly lower if they had been khaki, field grey or canary yellow? Not very likely.[146] However, especially in the Ardennes, a large number of the engagements that day took place in the forest or the undergrowth. When a soldier is caught in the line of fire amid foliage, it would certainly seem to be preferable to be dressed in field grey rather than bright colours.

On 22 August, the Germans reacted much more rapidly and effectively than the French to the surprise of the battles of encounter. Typically, two long columns of combatants and equipment advanced towards each other, often in fog and through regions whose relief rarely offered views over any great distance. The differing approaches of the two sides in the course of these unexpected encounters would have grave consequences for the extent of losses in the successive battles. The Germans began moving into defensive formations almost immediately, with the men seeking out advantageous and protected firing positions. For the French, the fundamental military doctrine (the all-out offensive) combined with the specific instructions issued by GQG ('The enemy will be attacked wherever it can be found') to urge a rapid attack on the enemy, without devoting much effort to reconnoitring its positions or supporting the artillery's endeavours. The marked contrasts between the approaches adopted by the two adversaries would prove very detrimental to the French side.

Specifically, the difference in the use of artillery would work in the Germans' favour, especially due to the speed with which they were able to get their guns into position. As we have already noted, both sides were using field artillery, 75 mm for the French and 77 mm for the Germans. Although relatively lightweight, these artillery pieces required some time to get into firing position. Sites for the batteries needed to be selected; the guns needed to be moved over a terrain that made manoeuvring quite difficult; the munitions wagons also needed to be transported, and then the firing positions needed to be set and adjusted. All of this required, at best, a good half-hour or more. The side able to prepare itself first for firing enjoyed a major advantage. Its adversary, compelled to manoeuvre and get itself into fighting posture amid the disorder typical of these unexpected encounters opposing inexperienced troops then needed to do so completely exposed, under fire from modern artillery. XV Corps outside Morhange, the Colonial Corps at Rossignol, XVII Corps between Ochamps and Luchy, like others that day, would experience first-hand the fatal inadequacies of the French approach.

Another key explanation for the massive extent of losses was that too few officers took the initiative to order a retreat on 22 August, even when it was clearly necessary. Differences between the command methods used by the French and German armies in 1914 had a significant influence on the extent of losses on both sides. As German subalterns and non-commissioned officers were left considerable room for initiative, they were able to adapt their actions rather rapidly to the unexpected circumstances of the battles of encounter in the second half of August. In contrast, the French side was still wedded to the notion that all instructions needed to be transmitted to and from high levels in the hierarchy (and therefore, during the war of movement, over great distances). This was a slow and delicate process, hindering initiatives by officers on the battlefield, with disastrous consequences. Amid the confusion of the early offensives, the circumstances of the fighting led to a breakdown in the chain of command. As a result, paralysis threatened both the discipline and the courage of the French troops standing still under fire working against their survival. By way of example, this was the case for the 3rd Colonial Division at Rossignol. As the local command structure had become dysfunctional, there was no one among the subalterns or non-commissioned officers to order a life-saving retreat. The troops were therefore quickly enveloped, then annihilated.

In a more general sense, however, the French army sustained such heavy losses in August 1914 because it made no particular effort to minimize them. Death in battle was viewed then as a quasi-natural fatality. Today, French society fully expects soldiers killed in combat to be honoured almost individually. For example, on 10 August 2012, François Hollande interrupted his holidays at Fort de Brégançon, the official summer residence of French presidents, to pay official homage at a funeral ceremony for a member of the French mountain infantry, who had died in combat three days earlier in Kapisa province, Afghanistan.[147] In 1914, there was no such relationship between French society and its military casualties. Reducing at all costs the number of soldiers killed was neither an obligation nor a major priority. Seeking minimal losses would have been perceived as a sign of weakness, of faint-heartedness on the part of military leaders, likely to sap the courage of soldiers in combat. With time, French military leaders would eventually accept the idea that superior firepower would henceforth consistently win out over even the boldest of exploits. But, in August 1914, too many of them were convinced that victory would only be achieved by accepting heavy losses.

Pulled into the Twentieth Century

It is difficult not to be struck by the marked contrast between the far-reaching advances in technology during this period relating to war materiel and the rigidity of military systems of thought and organization. Put simply, it is as if all physical aspects (weapons, transportation and so on), in other words the 'hardware' involved in the war, had already made the leap into the twentieth century, whereas everything intellectual in nature (strategy, tactics, organization, ideals, and so on), hence the war's 'software', was still stuck in the nineteenth century. In their hands, the French military held machine guns, but in their heads they were still at Austerlitz. This disjointed situation would prove fatal. Of course, the American Civil War, the colonial wars, the Russo-Japanese War and the Balkan Wars had already directed attention to all the military consequences of technical progress, but not all the lessons had yet been drawn: they were deemed too intellectually disturbing, too discomfiting from an organizational perspective, and too costly to implement. Above all, there was one important unacknowledged factor: none of the conflicts just mentioned directly opposed armies consisting of Western Europeans. Military and political elites would therefore be inclined to look askance at any lessons that might reasonably have been gleaned. The catastrophes of the battles in the first weeks of the war would trigger, willingly and especially unwillingly, an adaptive process at all levels and in all areas. Understandably, this process would be neither universal nor instantaneous. Joffre's tactic of *grignotage* in 1915, the 'nibbling' of enemy forces through attrition, would make it the deadliest year of the war for the French.[148] Nevertheless, soon thereafter a French army uniformed, equipped, organized and commanded in an entirely different manner would succeed, but not without superhuman efforts, in wearing down a German adversary that had clearly been superior at the beginning of the conflict.

A CRITICAL LAPSE IN FRENCH COLLECTIVE MEMORY

During the First World War, military leaders did not have a clear vision of what was happening in the battle zones. Today's army commanders in developed countries have access, at any moment, to a full complement of data on any event, at nearly every site in a battlefield. Satellites, GPS, drones and video cameras on helmets, among other equipment, allow the military hierarchy (from the unit commander to the chief of the general staff) to monitor each engagement in real time on a computer screen.[149] Some operations, such as the firing of missiles, are carried out by 'pilots' located thousands of miles from the battlefield.

In August 1914, the use of telephones and radio devices as command, communication and control systems was still in the embryonic stage. Communications between Moltke and German army leaders were transmitted via Belgian switchboard operators. Moreover, army leaders were geographically distant from their soldiers. From the Trojan War until the advent of firearms, army leaders fought among their troops, if not in front of them. Compelled by firearms to abandon the front lines, leaders of the modern era, such as Napoleon, nonetheless remained on the edge of the battlefield, preferably looking over the proceedings from a certain height. From such a vantage point, they could visually monitor the development of the fighting and correspond with commanders in the field via messengers. By contrast, chiefs of staff in 1914 – Joffre just as much as Moltke – facing the need to monitor massive armies distributed over several hundred kilometres, tended to remain at an ever greater distance from the battle lines. Joffre had established his headquarters initially at Château-Thierry, Moltke first at Koblenz and then at Luxembourg. They could no longer directly monitor events as they unfolded and scarcely had the means to obtain this information. Most of the messages they received were brief reports written by their army commanders.[150] In keeping with his method and due to his natural tendency to mistrust those under his command, Joffre frequently dispatched liaison officers to visit his army commanders and, on occasion, made these trips in person, as he famously did to Lanrezac's headquarters. But there again, he was far from the action. Even if Joffre had received specific information in real time about what was happening on the front, one might legitimately wonder what kind of impression he might have formed as a result. Over the course of his already lengthy military career, he had in fact served as a battle commander. But this had been in Tonkin, Madagascar and equatorial Africa. Joffre had thus never had the opportunity to observe personally the greater density of firepower in battles between European troops. And never had he been able to obtain an indirect, even watered-down, perspective such as the one we can gain today through movies and television, for example. Lacking this prior experience, it was easier for him to attribute the tactical failure of his subordinates to the weaknesses of some of his troops and the incompetence of their immediate commanders.

The French army has never offered its own cogent explanation of the level of human losses during this particularly bloody period. In the 106 volumes of *Les Armées françaises dans la Grande Guerre*, a mere three paragraphs are devoted to the Battle of Rossignol.[151] For the French military leadership, the catastrophe was not the level of losses, but instead the retreat by their armies faced with the effectiveness of the

German offensives. And the problem was to find explanations for these withdrawals without laying blame on the general staff or its chief. At the time, the first indications about the failures, given by Joffre on 21 August to Messimy, the war minister, were typical in this respect. Certain troops were faulted for their supposed lack of courage, or their officers were criticized for their alleged command inadequacies.

Not surprisingly, the first response was to relieve some of the highest-ranking officers, including Lanrezac, the Fifth Army commander, and Ruffey, the Third Army commander. In addition to these two men, some fifteen army corps commanders would also be sacked. However, it is clear that their disgrace was not in any way tied to the level of losses sustained. It would not be until late 1915 that the highly unfavourable comparison between the territory won during the offensives in Artois and Champagne ordered by Joffre and the massive losses recorded would begin to impugn his credibility. The lack of awareness of the actual extent of losses among political officials in 1914 is particularly striking, in the absence of adequate information from GQG and the war ministry, but also due to their reluctance to raise the issue with conviction. In fact, Gérard Guicheteau and Jean-Claude Simoën relate that Raymond Poincaré, president of France at the time, personally demanded an accounting of losses from war minister Millerand following the offensives in Artois in spring 1915. Deeply disturbed by the figures provided, which it should be noted were far lower than those for August 1914, Poincaré commented as follows in his memoirs:

> Between 6 May and 15 June, there were 451 officers killed, 1,081 wounded and 139 missing, along with 12,095 soldiers killed, 49,097 wounded and 13,517 missing. From 16 to 18 June, there were fifty-three officers killed, 151 wounded and nineteen missing, together with 1,377 soldiers killed, 5,675 wounded and 2,527 missing. The German losses are said to be much greater, but this is

very little better than guesswork; and besides, the German army is much larger than ours.[152]

Gradually, the French military would begin to reason, if not in terms of the extent of losses, at least by including this factor as one of the elements on the basis of which the success of a strategic initiative should be judged. In 1915, some generals thus began to express, quite publicly, their doubts about the relevance of Joffre's *grignotage* strategy. But Joffre would not be replaced as chief of the general staff until late 1916, although not without retaining the highest honours: he was made a Marshal of France, thereby becoming the first to receive this distinction since 1870.[153] Neither his brief successor, General Robert Nivelle, nor the latter's key subordinate, Mangin, would be so decorated. The losses sustained during the assault on the Chemin des Dames would immediately precipitate Nivelle's downfall. Mangin, a general of recognized talent, had attracted attention for his particularly effective use of native African troops in military operations, although often with heavy casualties, earning him the nickname '*l'Homme qui broie du noir*' (a pun on an expression for one who broods, here readily understood to refer, quite literally, to a crusher of blacks). At the victory parade of 11 November 1919, Marshal Joffre was still the first to pass on horseback under the Arc de Triomphe. It is true that it would have been difficult for the political and military authorities to lay blame on the man who had been the leader of the French armies for more than half of the conflict. After the fact, the authorities preferred to find fault with a single concept, that of the all-out offensive, many of whose theorists, Colonel Loyzeau de Grandmaison first among them, had not survived the war. Attributing the catastrophic losses early in the war to the application of a faulty tactic was reductive, but satisfying, for the French military establishment. This also made possible the belief that the problem had been resolved with the introduction, between the two wars, of a new French military doctrine that it would hardly be caricature to describe as an 'all-out defensive' stance.

These battles of August 1914 would leave behind proportionately fewer direct witnesses than any other of the events during the war. In the First World War as a whole, nearly one out of five French infantry soldiers would be killed (18 per cent of the men in the troops, 22 per cent of the subalterns and non-commissioned officers). Fatally, this proportion would be much higher among the 800,000 active men in August 1914, thus the most likely to serve in combat that month. Not only did they take part in the war's bloodiest confrontations, but they were subsequently exposed to the risk of getting themselves killed at some point over the next fifty months. This has created an inevitable imbalance in terms of contributions to collective memory, with far fewer accounts of the first three months of the war than the last three, for example.

Specifically, in this same collective memory, the success of the Battle of the Marne gradually wiped out the failure of the Battle of the Frontiers. As the latter occurred two weeks before the former, this earlier event came to be considered merely an engagement serving to prepare the most emblematic French victory of the entire war. Its glory effectively dispelled the dark days of 20–24 August, which thus slipped into oblivion. And yet, even if the Battle of the Marne certainly put the nail in the coffin of the Schlieffen Plan, the withdrawing German troops held on to their full battle capacity, which they would clearly demonstrate over the next four years.

Ultimately, discussing the extent of French losses at the start of the First World War was and always will be difficult.

At the beginning of the conflict, the level of losses was not a priority concern, and it would be some time before it would be considered even a subject of interest. Broaching this subject is still difficult, because it leads to questions about the responsibilities of various parties. If the military doctrine of the period, the 1914 strategic plan, as well as the preparation and outfitting of troops can be blamed, what can be said about the responsibility of civil and military authorities? The determination of accountability should certainly have begun at the level of Joffre and Messimy. But it is clear that it would not have stopped there. It is easy to understand the reluctance of the committee formed by Maurice Viollette to release its findings in 1919. Even more poignantly, all this raises the issue of whether the war might have been won in a different manner, at a lower cost in terms of human lives. A thorny question for a nation just emerging from such extreme devastation, and one that would be hard to hear for a sorely tried population. Finally, if it is accepted that human losses ought to be part and parcel of any thinking about the conflict, what then does 'winning' a war really mean, especially one in which, on a front where the French directly faced the Germans in battle, the winner sustained twice as many losses as the enemy, who were thought to be vanquished, at least for the following twenty-one years?

Recalling the catastrophe experienced on 22 August 1914 by the French forces thus leads inexorably to the question of who won this war. A question to which it seems a response is only possible in the context of a genuine reflection on the exit from war between France and Germany. An exit from war that, as everyone recognizes now, did not actually take place in 1918, nor in 1945, since the cold war prolonged the conflict in another form. And one which was not really even achieved at the start of the 1990s, with the reunification of Germany. Can the upheavals currently shaking the Europe of institutions as well as its very economic and financial foundations, coupled with the approaching centenary of the European 'suicide' of 1914, provide the opportunity to exit this conflict at last? Such an outcome is certainly desirable. Among other interrogations, this will require a close examination of the conditions surrounding the First World War and the manner in which it was fought. One of the aims of this volume is to contribute, however modestly, to this debate.

EPILOGUE

ROSSIGNOL, 23 JUNE 2012

A gently climbing road leads to the village of Rossignol after crossing the Semois at Breuvanne. The river is quite narrow. This bridge, where so many French soldiers lost their lives on 22 August 1914 trying to cross the river under continuous shelling, cannot be much more than twenty metres long, but the riverbed seems deep enough that it would be impossible to ford, if not by foot soldiers alone, at least when you consider that they would have needed to manoeuvre the horse-drawn artillery and supply wagons. Leaving the bridge behind, the road curves to the north-west, bordered here and there by a few farms and a number of pastures protected by barbed-wire fences. The village church is at the centre of Rossignol's main square. Its white walls still bear the traces of unexploded German shells. On this early summer morning, the stillness of the village is disturbed only by the constant stream of tractors and other farm equipment hard at work everywhere.

Heading north from the main square on foot, in the direction of Neufchâteau, we soon reach the spot where the French 3rd

Colonial Infantry Division ran up against the German 9th Infantry Division. But first we find ourselves on a narrow, unbending street whose sign, reading 'Rue de l'Ancienne Voie Romaine', stirs his curiosity. After leaving the village, this little thoroughfare continues absolutely straight into the forest, dissolving into the distant horizon. It is in fact a Roman road, built to move troop reinforcements quickly between Gaul's garrisons and the Roman fortresses along the Rhine. Two thousand years later, the geographical constraints governing the choice of invasion routes remained the same. In August 1914, after crossing the Rhine opposite Liège to invade Belgium and then France, it was best to follow precisely this very road built by Roman soldiers through the forest to supply the fortified sites intended, already then, to prevent the Germanic tribes from crossing the Rhine.

Lost in reflections on the Roman notion of *limes*, or 'boundary marker', and the idea of the frontier, with visions of the cohorts of Roman legions, in whose footsteps we are treading, passing before our eyes, we are surprised to arrive so quickly at the forest separating Rossignol from Neufchâteau, where the Chasseurs d'Afrique had run after the first German Uhlans encountered at daybreak on the main square of the village. In perhaps no more than ten minutes, we have walked the entire length of the fields over which the German troops had advanced slowly, in the afternoon, to envelop the French soldiers incapacitated under a deluge of shells at Rossignol. After about another kilometre, we reach the edge of the forest where hundreds of French riflemen were mowed down as they charged madly, bayonets at the ready. Entering the forest, instantly rather thick with growth, everything goes quite dark, and our eyes need a moment to adjust. The road through the forest is straight but narrow, no more than four metres wide, bordered by wet ditches. The undergrowth is very dense, which would make it difficult to see anything on either side of the road, even a rapid and massive advance on our right or left. Nevertheless, it is here that two colonial infantry regiments charged, one after the other, on the morning of 22 August. Instantly, we are struck by the natural confinement of this battlefield: the boundaries of these killing fields are extraordinarily limited. Any troop entering this forest would quickly find itself trapped in a cone-shaped area just a few dozen metres at its base and just slightly more than one hundred metres deep.

Any visitor would very likely react with disbelief, as we did, when considering the nature of the battle French soldiers were ordered to wage that day. From this vantage point, it is easy to imagine German soldiers lying in wait in the ditches, at the edge of the woods, and along the road leading into the forest. Without needing to dig trenches, the undulating and rough terrain would have offered them stable, well-dispersed and relatively protected positions from which to fire their weapons. On that fateful day, they were able to position themselves just a few dozen metres from the grouped enemy forces, who were visible and exposed, and themselves experienced great difficulty in locating their adversaries through the trees and bushes. It does not seem necessary to have completed extensive military training to realize that, under these circumstances, it would have been impossible for an infantry troop to charge massively, bayonets at the ready, without being massacred. Huddled on such a narrow road, the men would have been swallowed up inside a veritable sinkhole of dense and continuous fire. Individual accounts of the day's events confirm this assessment: it was precisely the opinion of all those who had initially entered the forest and managed to emerge, from the first Chasseurs d'Afrique, chasing the Uhlans who had left Rossignol so quickly, to the officers of the 1st Colonial Infantry Regiment. But no one listened to them. Irrational orders continued to be given, and followed. Over several hours, successive groups of French soldiers stormed the forest, heading to certain death. And yet the organizational and technical processes of a military concentration that had made it possible to bring men who were still in their barracks or behind their ploughs just three weeks before had been a model of modern efficiency and rationality. But, at the other end of the chain, at the moment of confrontation, this same rationality seems to have disappeared, among the leaders as among the rank and file.

As if better to underscore the ultimate consequence of these preposterous tactical choices, it is precisely here, on the left side of the road just outside the forest, that the main French military cemetery bringing together the battle dead was built. The other burial site is found a few hundred metres away, within the forest, on the other side of this straight and narrow road gently climbing to the north. Within these two cemeteries are grouped the graves of French soldiers that, during the war and its immediate aftermath, had been scattered across nine sites in proximity to where the men had fallen. Flanked at its entrance by a monument to the Colonial Corps soldiers, the cemetery at the edge of the forest, like the second one, includes several hundred tombs marked with little white crosses, distributed over the three levels of the slightly sloping terrain. Many names inscribed on these crosses clearly seem to be of Breton origin, which is hardly surprising since the two regiments of the 3rd Colonial Infantry Division were stationed on the Atlantic coast, at Brest, Cherbourg and Rochefort. The number of crosses in evidence, several hundred in each cemetery, does not appear to reflect accurately the thousands of Frenchmen killed on 22 August. But when we walk towards the rear of the cemetery at the edge of the forest, we find an unadorned stela bearing the following inscription: 'Here lie 1,108 unknown French soldiers and officers, who died for France.' Most of those killed were not able to be identified individually. Once the fighting had ended, the German troops had quickly buried the cadavers, very near to where they had fallen, as they would have begun to decompose very rapidly in the August heat. Then the front quickly moved to the south, and with it the attention of the military authorities. By 1919, when the French authorities began to search systematically for buried soldiers and exhume the bodies, identification had become very difficult, especially since soldiers in 1914 had not been equipped with metallic identity badges, but simply with individual cardboard tags, sometimes rolled up inside tiny glass bottles. When it was possible, the dead were more often identified from their personal effects (journals, name tags on clothing and so on). Since regimental insignia worn at the collar held up better, many of the crosses indicate a rank and regiment, but not a name. Numerous families obtained the right to repatriate the bodies of their loved ones home to France. In contrast, for the most part, the authorities preferred that soldiers who died for France on French territory be buried at the battle sites, which explains the huge cemeteries in the Somme, Champagne, Artois and Verdun and the prevalence of monuments to the fallen, substituting for individual tombs in the native towns and villages of soldiers and officers throughout the rest of the country. For the soldiers killed in Belgium, the families were free to repatriate the bodies, if desired, and it is thought that this was the case for at least 30 to 40 per cent of the identified victims.

Despite the natural homogeneity of the white crosses, the landscape of these tombs is quite often broken up by individualistic elements. Here and there, we spot fresh or artificial flowers, small plaques, notes, reminding us that these soldiers were also sons, brothers, fathers, lovers and spouses, and that the projectiles that took their lives devastated other lives as effectively as a burst of shrapnel.

At the entrance to the cemetery on the edge of the forest, in front of the monument to the Colonial Corps soldiers, a noticeboard recounts, in French, English and German, the circumstances behind its creation. The monument, as well as the organization and renovation of both cemeteries at the forest of Neufchâteau, owes a great deal to the dedication of one individual, a veteran and industrialist from Lorraine by the name of Paul Feunette. Feunette had a son named Gabriel, aged twenty-one in 1914, who was brilliant yet temperamental. Interested in giving his son a leg up in life, Feunette used his connections to obtain a position for Gabriel in the third regiment of the Chasseurs d'Afrique, a cavalry unit known for its military rigour, which was part of the Colonial Corps. Feunette received his son's last letter, full of enthusiasm for the battle ahead, following the announcement of his death outside Rossignol on 22 August. After the war, Feunette moved heaven and earth to honour Gabriel's memory and that of his comrades in arms. A prestigious committee was formed, under the patronage of Albert I of Belgium and the French prime minister Aristide Briand, which raised considerable funds. On 22 August 1927, the monument was unveiled at a ceremony attended by several thousand people. The next year, on the anniversary of the battle, Feunette returned to pay his respects at his son's grave. Then he killed himself with a shot to the head.

In that summer of 2012, leaving the cemetery slowly, words escaped me as I turned to look back so often that I found myself nearly walking backwards. My own twenty-one-year-old son was at my side, fully realizing that he was accompanying his father in nothing less than a pilgrimage. Our shoulders were weighed down by the raw sadness that continued to filter into the air from the modest graves of so many brave men.

ACKNOWLEDGEMENTS

'Although you might think you'll be writing a history book about 1914, you'll be surprised to discover how much it'll be about you!'

This was the response of one of my friends when I told him of my plans as a fledgling author, then very much in the embryonic stage, a friend whose long list of published titles, each more moving and thought-provoking than the last, not to mention the strong bond of friendship between us, was enough to give me pause. Several months later, as I am tying up the loose ends of a text hatched arduously by someone for whom writing is not a profession, and still less something that comes easily, I realize that he was right.

This book would never have seen the light of day were it not for the intelligence and devotion of my loving wife, who knew just when to push me ahead, and then help me stay the course, on the long and winding road I viewed before me with apprehension.

While on this path, I have been guided, pulled, goaded onwards, accompanied, read and encouraged by so many people both within and outside the EHESS that I can only acknowledge my debt of gratitude to a single one, Stéphane

Audoin-Rouzeau, of course, and all the others through him. I was also lucky enough to meet at my French publisher, Fayard, an editor, Sophie Kucoyannis, who knows how to combine attention, rigour and warmth in an ideal way. However, any imperfections, inadequacies, errors or omissions in this text are mine, and mine alone.

BIBLIOGRAPHY

Ardant du Picq, Charles, Études sur le *combat: combat antique et combat modern* (Paris: Chapelot, 1903).

Audoin-Rouzeau, Stéphane, *L'enfant de l'ennemi, 1914–1918: viol, avortement, infanticide pendant la Grande Guerre* (Paris: Aubier, 1995).

——— 'Artillerie et mitrailleuses', in Stéphane Audoin-Rouzeau and Jean-Jacques Becker, eds, *Encyclopédie de la Grande Guerre, 1914–1918: histoire et culture* (Paris: Bayard, 2004), pp. 255–61.

——— *Les armes et la chair: trois objets de mort en 1914–1918* (Paris: Armand Colin, 2009).

Bach, André, *Fusillés pour l'exemple: 1914–1915* (Paris: Tallandier, 2003).

Baldin, Damien, and Emmanuel Saint-Fuscien, *Charleroi, 21–23 août 1914* (Paris: Tallandier, 2012).

Becker, Jean-Jacques, 'Entrées en guerre', in Stéphane Audoin-Rouzeau and Jean-Jacques Becker, eds, *Encyclopédie de la Grande Guerre, 1914–1918: histoire et culture* (Paris: Bayard, 2004), pp. 193–202.

Bley, Helmut, *South-West Africa under German Rule, 1894–1914* (Evanston, IL: Northwestern University Press, 1971).

Buat, Edmond, *L'armée allemande pendant la guerre de 1914–1918* (Paris: Chapelot, 1920).

Clayton, Anthony, *Paths of Glory: The French Army, 1914–18* (London: Cassell, 2005).

Cosson, Olivier, 'La « Grande Guerre » imaginée des officiers français: combat, représentations et anticipation autour de la guerre russo-japonaise', in Christophe Prochasson and Anne Rasmussen, eds, *Vrai et faux dans la Grande Guerre* (Paris: La Découverte, 2004), pp. 133–51.

Delaporte, Sophie, *Les médecins dans la Grande Guerre* (Paris: Bayard, 2003).

Doughty, Robert A., *Pyrrhic Victory: French Strategy and Operations in the Great War* (Cambridge, MA: Harvard University Press, 2008).

Enseignements de la guerre russo-japonaise [located at Service Historique de l'Armée de Terre (SHAT), ref. 7N 1532-1533-1534].

Failin, Paul, 'Cahiers du Caporal-clairon Paul Failin du 3° R.I.C.' Available at https://sites.google.com/site/amicaledu3rima/le-regiment/historique/centenaire-2eme-partie.

Ferguson, Niall, *The Pity of War* (London: Penguin, 1998).

Garros, Louis, 'Le corps d'armée colonial sur la Semoy: la bataille de Rossignol (22 août 1914)'. Text of the presentation made by Lieutenant Garros to the Cercle Militaire de Rouen, 25 June 1929. Available at http://67400.free.fr/colonial_sur_la_Semoy.htm.

Gewald, Jan-Bart, *Herero Heroes: A Socio-political History of the Herero of Namibia, 1890–1923* (Athens, OH: Ohio University Press, 1998).

Grandmaison, Louis Loyzeau de, *Le dressage de l'infanterie en vue du combat offensif* (Paris: Berger-Levrault, 1906).

Grasset, Alphonse Louis, *La guerre en action, surprise d'une division Rossignol-Saint Vincent (22 août 1914)* (Paris: Berger-Levrault, 1932).

Gudmundsson, Bruce, 'Unexpected Encounter at Bertrix', in

Robert Cowley, ed., *The Great War: Perspectives on the First World War* (New York: Random House, 2003), pp. 21–xx.

Guicheteau, Gérard, and Jean-Claude Simoën, *Les années sanglantes, 1914–1918* (Paris: Fayard, 2006).

Hanson, Victor Davis, *The Western Way of War: Infantry Battle in Classical Greece* (New York: Knopf, 1989).

Herwig, Holger H., *The Marne, 1914: The Opening of World War I and the Battle That Changed the World* (New York: Random House, 2009).

Horne, John, and Alan Kramer, *German Atrocities, 1914: A History of Denial* (New Haven, CT: Yale University Press, 2001).

Hull, Isabel V., *Absolute Destruction: Military Culture and the Practices of War in Imperial Germany* (Ithaca, NY: Cornell University Press, 2005).

Keegan, John, *The Face of Battle* (Harmondsworth: Penguin, 1983).

Langle de Cary, Fernand Louis Armand Marie de, *Souvenirs de commandement, 1914–1916* (Paris: Payot, 1935).

Laurens, Louis, 'Récit du combat de Rossignol par le commandant Laurens (capitaine à l'E.M. de la 3° DIC le 22 août 1914)', *Avenir du Luxembourg* (9 September 1921). Available at https://www.histoire-genealogie.com/Fin-1917-Victor-Latour-retrouve?lang=fr.

Lefebvre, Georges, *La Grande Peur de 1789* (Paris: Armand Colin, 1932).

Le Naour, Jean-Yves, *Désunion nationale: la légende noire des soldats du Midi* (Paris: Vendémiaire, 2011).

Le Nen, Nicolas, *Task Force Tiger: journal de marche d'un chef de corps français en Afghanistan* (Paris: Economica, 2010).

'Massacre de Tamines', Wikipedia. Available at http://fr.wikipedia.org/wiki/Massacre_de_Tamines.

Ministère de la guerre, État-major des Armées, Service

historique, *Les armées françaises dans la Grande Guerre* (Paris: Imprimerie Nationale, 1922).

Moreau, Jean, Éric Labayle and Jean-Louis Philippart, *Rossignol, 22 août 1914: journal du commandant Jean Moreau, chef d'état-major de la 3e division coloniale: suivi des témoignages du lieutenant Chaumel et du colonel Guichard-Montguers* (Parçay-sur-Vienne: Anovi, 2002).

Mosier, John, *The Myth of the Great War: A New Military History of World War I* (New York: HarperCollins, 2001).

Mosse, George L., *Fallen Soldiers: Reshaping the Memory of the World Wars* (New York: Oxford University Press, 1990).

Psichari, Ernest, *L'appel des armes* (Paris: G. Oudin, 1913).

Saint-Fuscien, Emmanuel, *À vos ordres? La relation d'autorité dans l'armée française de la Grande Guerre* (Paris: Éditions de l'EHESS, 2011).

Stenographische Berichte über die Verhandlungen des Deutschen Reichstages [Stenographic minutes of German Reichstag debates], vol. 202, p. 4104 (30 January 1905).

Tucker, Spencer C., ed., *The Encyclopedia of the Spanish–American and Philippine–American Wars: A Political, Social, and Military History* (Santa Barbara, CA: ABC-CLIO, 2009).

Tyng, Sewell T., *The Campaign of the Marne, 1914* (Yardley, PA: Westholme, 2007).

Vigarello, Georges, *Le corps redressé: histoire d'un pouvoir pédagogique* (Paris: Armand Colin, 2001).

White, Matthew, 'Source List and Detailed Death Tolls for the Primary Megadeaths of the Twentieth Century'. Available at http://necrometrics.com/20c5m.htm.

Wilhelm II, 'Hun Speech' [1900], trans. Thomas Dunlap, GHDI [website]. Speech given by Kaiser Wilhelm II at Bremerhaven on 27 July 1990. Available at http://germanhistorydocs.ghi-dc.org/sub_document.cfm?document_id=755&language=english.

Winter, Jay, 'Demography', in John Horne, ed., *A Companion to World War I* (Malden, MA: Wiley-Blackwell, 2010), pp. 248–62.

Winter, Jay, and Blaine Baggett, *The Great War and the Shaping of the Twentieth Century* (New York: Penguin Studio, 1996).

Zuber, Terence, *The Battle of the Frontiers: Ardennes, 1914* (Charleston, SC: History Press, 2007).

TABLES AND APPENDICES

Table 1

Military participation and military losses in the First World War

Country	Mobilized	Dead	Wounded	Prisoners/ Missing	Casualties	% of Mobilized
Allied Forces						
Russia	15,798,000	1,800,000	4,950,000	2,500,000	9,250,000	59%
France	7,891,000	1,375,800	4,266,000	537,000	6,178,800	78%
British Empire and Dominions	8,904,467	908,371	2,090,212	191,652	3,190,235	36%
Italy	5,615,000	578,000	947,000	600,000	2,125,000	38%
United States	4,273,000	114,000	234,000	4,526	352,526	8%
Japan	800,000	300	907	3	1,210	0%
Romania	1,000,000	250,706	120,000	80,000	450,706	45%
Serbia	750,000	278,000	133,148	15,958	427,106	57%
Belgium	365,000	38,716	44,686	34,659	118,061	32%
Greece	353,000	26,000	21,000	1,000	48,000	14%
Portugal	100,000	7,222	13,751	12,318	33,291	33%
Montenegro	50,000	3,000	10,000	7,000	20,000	40%
Total	45,899,467	5,380,115	12,830,704	3,984,116	22,194,935	48%

Country	Mobilized	Dead	Wounded	Prisoners/ Missing	Casualties	% of Mobilized
Central Powers						
Germany	13,200,000	2,037,000	4,216,058	1,152,800	7,405,858	56%
Austria-Hungary	9,000,000	1,100,000	3,620,000	2,200,000	6,920,000	77%
Turkey	2,998,000	804,000	400,000	250,000	1,454,000	48%
Bulgaria	400,000	87,500	152,390	27,029	266,919	67%
Total	25,598,000	4,028,500	8,388,448	3,629,829	16,046,777	63%
Grand Total	71,497,467	9,408,615	21,219,152	7,613,945	38,241,712	53%

Source: Jay Winter, 'Demography', in John Horne, ed., *A Companion to World War I* (Malden, MA: Wiley-Blackwell, 2010), p. 249.

TABLE 2

APPROXIMATE FIGURES FOR THE NUMBER OF DEAD BY MONTH AND BY YEAR

	January	February	March	April	May	June	July	August	September	October	November	December	Number of Dead per Year	Percentage of Total
1914								84,500	99,000	46,000	38,300	33,300	301,100	23.60%
1915	25,400	23,500	28,500	27,700	41,600	43,400	22,400	10,500	59,700	37,600	7,800	5,600	333,700	26.20%
1916	7,900	14,200	19,400	17,800	24,000	26,600	30,500	20,600	35,100	23,600	13,600	10,400	243,700	19.00%
1917	5,400	5,700	9,700	40,700	25,900	10,400	11,500	14,900	10,800	10,800	4,700	3,900	154,400	12.10%
1918: up to November 11 inclusive	3,400	4,100	9,000	17,500	20,500	22,200	29,600	29,000	22,000	37,400	7,900		202,600	15.90%
After November 11, 1918												26,300	26,300	2.10%

This table summarizes the information provided on the site www.grande-guerre-1418.com. In order to arrive at the monthly figures for the number of deaths on the French side, the developers of this site analyzed the data sheets filed by the French war ministry at the time, which may be consulted on the 'Mémoire des Hommes' site of the French defense ministry (www.memoiredeshommes.sga.defense.gouv.fr). Even though the total derived from the database records is slightly lower that the total estimate of losses, given the number of personnel missing in action, duplicates, illegible records, etc., the proportional breakdown by month seems reliable.

APPENDIX 1

FRENCH MILITARY ORGANIZATION IN AUGUST 1914

The military organization used in France has changed frequently, and the one in place in August 1914 was the result of the coming into effect of a law extending the term of mandatory military service from two to three years and the implementation of 'Plan XVII' for mobilization. The aim of this section is to outline the architecture of this organization at the very beginning of the war, and the corresponding orders of magnitude of each category of personnel.

ARMY CORPS

The fundamental unit of the French military organization in August 1914, each army corps comprised 40,000 men, about 30,000 of whom served as combatants.

These forces included, in principle, two active infantry divisions, to which were added a cavalry regiment, a cavalry corps artillery (2,000 men and 2,000 horses), as well as a general staff, engineers, medical and veterinary staff, the commissariat, and so on.

In 1914, the mobilized were divided into twenty-one army corps, including the Colonial Corps.

INFANTRY DIVISION

In 1914, the strength of an infantry division was 15,500 men, including 280 officers.

Each division had two brigades of three regiments. To these forces were added a divisional artillery (1,600 men and thirty-six 75-mm field guns), a cavalry squadron (150 men), and a company of engineers. In all, there were forty-six active infantry divisions at the start of the war; some of these divisions were independent and thus were not attached to any specific army corps. This was the case for the 37th and 38th Infantry Divisions, consisting of Tunisians and Algerians, and the 43rd Infantry Division (and later the 44th Infantry Division as well), bringing together the mountain infantry troops.

INFANTRY REGIMENT

In August 1914, there were a total of 173 active infantry regiments, each with a standard complement of 113 officers and 3,226 soldiers. Each regiment included three battalions.

BATTALION

A battalion consisted of some 1,000 men divided into four companies of about 250 soldiers each. Each company was itself divided into four sections commanded by a first (or second) lieutenant.

There were a certain number of departures from this basic organization, relating to the special status of some units (colonial troops, *chasseurs*) or the use of reserve units after the general mobilization.

For example, the Colonial Corps had three rather than two divisions. In addition, its constituent elements at each echelon had distinctive names, indicating their allegiance to the Colonial Corps (for example, 3rd Colonial Infantry Division, 1st Colonial Infantry Regiment, or 1st Colonial Corps Artillery Regiment).

Similarly, the *chasseurs*, whether on foot or on horseback, were organized differently from other units. Their distinctive characteristic, which encouraged their development in the nineteenth century, was that they were not intended to fight in lines, but instead in small mobile groups; thus they used an organization suited to this purpose, with the battalion as their fundamental unit, consisting of about 1,700 men.

As reservists were called up, reserve battalions were added to the active units, also using a different organization. For example, a reserve regiment included only two battalions.

APPENDIX 2

'LES RAISONS DU DÉSASTRE'

From Fernand Louis Armand Marie de Langle de Cary, *Souvenirs de commandement*, 1914–1916 (Paris: Payot, 1935)

29 September 1914: For today's entry, I thought it would be useful to cast a backward glance over the events since 4 August. What a wealth of lessons can be drawn from these eight weeks of war!

Our early failures seem to have been due in the first place to a defective operations plan: attacking with both wings at the same time, in Lorraine and in Belgium. This process, which is akin to the German doctrine developed by Schlieffen, can only work if our forces are far greater in number than those of the enemy. But this was not the case. To make matters worse, this disparity was even more severe than we had originally thought. The Germans managed nearly to double the strength of all their army corps, while maintaining their fighting capacity;

they attacked us with thirty-four active or reserve corps. Only four active corps were left along the Russian frontier.

Our attack in Lorraine ran up against powerful defensive forces already fully combat-ready in peacetime just a few miles from the border: hence our defeats at Morhange and in the Vosges. Thanks to the qualities of our leaders and the courage of our troops, we were able to redress these defeats and break the counter-offensive by the enemy, who was trying to outflank our right wing. But at what cost! We could have halted its advance in Lorraine, by remaining in an active and vigilant defensive posture while we were attacking in Belgium. In this way, the result we would have obtained after the defeats at Morhange and in the Vosges would have been easier and less costly, leaving the troops intact! For the enemy, this would probably have meant defeat and a definitive withdrawal rather than merely being stopped. Besides, the Lorraine offensive could not bring us any decisive outcome, with Metz and Strasbourg on our flanks and a narrow field of action through the Vosges and the Étangs region on the one hand, and between the latter and the entrenched camp at Metz on the other.

The operations plan was entirely the work of General Joffre and his general staff. It was not submitted for review and approval by the Supreme War Council. Most of the army commanders, myself included, were only familiar with the concentration plans as they related to their own armies; we had no knowledge of the chief of staff's intentions. His method is to develop his strategies supported only by his immediate entourage, without consulting his army commanders, without even keeping them informed of his plans other than by way of the instructions and orders he sends to them. I'm not criticizing this method per se, but in my view a collaborative style is preferable, building relationships based on mutual trust. This would not in any way diminish the authority of the supreme leader, who always has the final say.

ENDNOTES

1 John Horne and Alan Kramer, *German Atrocities, 1914: A History of Denial* (New Haven, CT: Yale University Press, 2001).
2 Damien Baldin and Emmanuel Saint-Fuscien, *Charleroi, 21–23 août 1914* (Paris: Tallandier, 2012).
3 Georges Vigarello, *Le corps redressé: histoire d'un pouvoir pédagogique* (Paris: Armand Colin, 2001).
4 Here we turn on its head the title of a work by Henry Rousso, *La dernière catastrophe: l'histoire, le présent, le contemporain* (Paris: Gallimard, 2013).
5 Marc Bloch, *L'étrange défaite: témoignage écrit en 1940* (Paris: Gallimard, 1990).
6 Jay Winter and Blaine Baggett, *The Great War and the Shaping of the Twentieth Century* (New York: Penguin Studio, 1996).
7 Ibid., p. 68.
8 Matthew White, 'Source List and Detailed Death Tolls for the Primary Megadeaths of the Twentieth Century'. Available at http://necrometrics.com/20c5m.htm.
9 In June 1973, when I received my diploma from

Sciences Po, France had only 250,000 unemployed, a figure that had passed the 3 million mark by 2012.
10 Victor Davis Hanson, *The Western Way of War: Infantry Battle in Classical Greece* (New York: Knopf, 1989).
11 'Poilu' – meaning, literally, 'hairy one' – is an informal term for a French infantryman, particularly one who served in the First World War.
12 A century earlier, some 6,800 of the 70,000 troops taken into battle by Napoleon at Waterloo on 18 June 1815 were killed or died of their wounds.
13 Every year on 1 July, today more than ever, hundreds of British visitors assemble at dawn on the battlefields – and cemeteries – of the region to commemorate the opening of the British infantry assault and the fallen soldiers.
14 As shown in Table 1, more than one in three Serbians mobilized were killed over the course of the war, versus fewer than one in four of their French counterparts.
15 See Niall Ferguson, The Pity of War (London: Penguin, 1998), pp. 290–314.
16 This indisputable fact gave rise to the specious notion, widely held in Germany's right-wing circles after 1918, that the German army had not been defeated militarily but had instead been 'stabbed in the back' by republican politicians and their supporters.
17 For an analysis of the preparation of artillery for the Battle of the Somme in 1916, see John Keegan, The Face of Battle (Harmondsworth: Penguin, 1983).
18 So many generals were sacked that the new verb *limoger*, and thus the corresponding noun *limogeage*, entered the French language, and are still used colloquially to refer to the act of removing someone from office for incompetence and any removal of this type, respectively.

19 See Appendix 1 for a discussion of French military organization in 1914.
20 André Bach, *Fusillés pour l'exemple: 1914–1915* (Paris: Tallandier, 2003), p. 275.
21 See Jean-Yves Le Naour, *Désunion nationale: la légende noire des soldats du Midi* (Paris: Vendémiaire, 2011).
22 In fact, this expression seems to have been first used by a Russian officer in 1855 during the Crimean War, circulated at the time in British newspapers, to describe the failed attempt by British troops to storm the fortress of Sevastopol.
23 In 1914, an infantry regiment numbered about 3,400 men organized into three battalions.
24 Jean Moreau, Éric Labayle and Jean-Louis Philippart, Rossignol, *22 août 1914: journal du commandant Jean Moreau, chef d'état-major de la 3e division coloniale: suivi des témoignages du lieutenant Chaumel et du colonel Guichard-Montguers* (Parçay-sur-Vienne: Anovi, 2002), pp. 60–6.
25 Ibid.
26 Discharged for ill health and transferred to Switzerland, he succumbed to tuberculosis there in 1917.
27 Moreau, Labayle and Philippart, Rossignol, *22 août 1914*, pp. 70–2.
28 Henri Ey, *Manuel de Psychiatrie* (Paris: Masson, 2010), pp. 192–5.
29 See Chapter 8.
30 Ernest Psichari, *L'appel des armes* (Paris: G. Oudin, 1913).
31 Recalling the celebrated painting by Alphonse de Neuville, *Les dernières cartouches* (The last cartridges), an omnipresent image of the Franco-Prussian War during this period.
32 Paul Failin, 'Cahiers du Caporal-clairon Paul Failin du 3° R.I.C.' Available at https://sites.google.com/site/amicaledu3rima/le-regiment/historique/centenaire-2eme-partie. These notes, written about fifteen years

	after taking part in the battle, cover Corporal Failin's recollections from his mobilization until being taken prisoner by the Germans on 13 January 1915.
33	Ibid.
34	Alphonse Louis Grasset, *La guerre en action, surprise d'une division Rossignol-Saint Vincent (22 août 1914)* (Paris: Berger-Levrault, 1932).
35	Louis Laurens, 'Récit du combat de Rossignol par le commandant Laurens (capitaine à l'E.M. de la 3° DIC le 22 août 1914)', *Avenir du Luxembourg* (9 September 1921). Available at https://www.histoire-genealogie.com/Fin-1917-Victor-Latour-retrouve?lang=fr.
36	Louis Garros, 'Le corps d'armée colonial sur la Semoy: la bataille de Rossignol (22 août 1914)'. Text of the presentation made by Lieutenant Garros to the Cercle Militaire de Rouen, 25 June 1929. Available at http://67400.free.fr/colonial_sur_la_Semoy.htm.
37	The barbed wire was very likely installed by local people, and thus well before the battle.
38	Fernand Louis Armand Marie de Langle de Cary, *Souvenirs de commandement, 1914–1916* (Paris: Payot, 1935).
39	Terence Zuber, *The Battle of the Frontiers: Ardennes, 1914* (Charleston, SC: History Press, 2007).
40	See Chapter 8 for a discussion of this term and its complex significance for German troops in 1914.
41	These Rossignol civilians were thus the first Europeans in the twentieth century to be shipped eastward in cattle cars by Germans to be killed.
42	Bismarck viewed the return of these lands as a simple annulment of Louis XIV's annexations under the Peace of Westphalia in 1648, which brought an end to the Thirty Years War.
43	This was a period when the French treasury, whose revenue consisted uniquely of indirect taxes, had difficulty financing investments in public infrastructure.

44 Edmond Buat, *L'armée allemande pendant la guerre de 1914–1918* (Paris: Chapelot, 1920).

45 Given rapid advances in the destructive power of weapons during the last third of the nineteenth century, this view was as widely held at the time as today's belief that nuclear war is an impossibility.

46 Thus contrasting with the French rail network, all of whose lines radiate from Paris.

47 All members of Schlieffen's general staff were strongly urged to familiarize themselves fully with the text in which he had laid out most of his ideas on military theory, entitled simply Cannae.

48 Holger H. Herwig, *The Marne, 1914: The Opening of World War I and the Battle That Changed the World* (New York: Random House, 2009), pp. 41–4.

49 An oft-repeated anecdote, perhaps apocryphal, recounts that Schlieffen's last words on his death bed were 'Keep the right wing strong!'

50 Anthony Clayton, *Paths of Glory: The French Army, 1914–18* (London: Cassell, 2005), p. 35.

51 Sewell T. Tyng, *The Campaign of the Marne, 1914* (Yardley, PA: Westholme, 2007), pp. 13–14.

52 Louis Loyzeau de Grandmaison, *Le dressage de l'infanterie en vue du combat offensif* (Paris: Berger-Levrault, 1906).

53 Charles Ardant du Picq, *Études sur le combat: combat antique et combat modern* (Paris: Chapelot, 1903).

54 Emmanuel Saint-Fuscien, *À vos ordres? La relation d'autorité dans l'armée française de la Grande Guerre* (Paris: Éditions de l'EHESS, 2011).

55 *Enseignements de la guerre russo-japonaise* [located at Service Historique de l'Armée de Terre (SHAT), ref. 7N 1532-1533-1534].

56 Olivier Cosson, 'La « Grande Guerre » imaginée des officiers français: combat, représentations et anticipation autour de la guerre russo-japonaise', in Christophe Prochasson and Anne Rasmussen,

eds, *Vrai et faux dans la Grande Guerre* (Paris: La Découverte, 2004).
57 Quoted ibid..
58 Herwig, *The Marne, 1914*, pp. 55–6.
59 Tyng, *The Campaign of the Marne, 1914*, pp. 13–14.
60 Due to the increasing distance from which lines of infantrymen exchanged rifle fire, the shooters were less and less able to ascertain whether they had effectively reached their targets. By the same token, many soldiers were not immediately aware, especially near the beginning of the war, that an enemy, frequently outside their visual range, was firing on them.
61 The English tradition stressing the importance of the accurate firing of rifles grew out of the important place held by archery in English culture as far back as the Middle Ages. In fact, a royal order in 1363 required all Englishmen to practise the sport on Sundays and holidays.
62 Stéphane Audoin-Rouzeau, 'Artillerie et mitrailleuses', in Stéphane Audoin-Rouzeau and Jean-Jacques Becker, eds, *Encyclopédie de la Grande Guerre, 1914–1918: histoire et culture* (Paris: Bayard, 2004).
63 The massive popularity of today's video games, which very often include simulated firing of weapons with hyper-realistic effects, offers an interesting contemporary perspective on the attraction the manning of machine guns would have had in the early years of the last century. Physicians and video-game developers have noted the addictive nature of these 'games', especially among young men, where the aim is to mow down successive waves of virtual adversaries. Biologists have found that levels of dopamine, a hormone associated with the brain's reward-oriented pleasure system, increase rapidly in video-game players. When dopamine levels rise quickly, a rush of pleasure is experienced, but when

	the expected reward is not delivered (when the player does not return to the game), dopamine release is inhibited, creating the opposite sensation and thus strong cravings for the source of the addiction.
64	Stéphane Audoin-Rouzeau, *Les armes et la chair: trois objets de mort en 1914–1918* (Paris: Armand Colin, 2009), pp. 15–17.
65	At a distance of six kilometres, a difference of one degree in the positioning of a gun compared to the previous shot entailed a 200-metre discrepancy on impact.
66	John Mosier, *The Myth of the Great War: A New Military History of World War I* (New York: HarperCollins, 2001), p. 41.
67	With considerable heating of the barrel and a risk of rapidly exhausting the supply of ammunition. The normal rate of fire was about fifteen rounds per minute, which is already high. Earlier models of lightweight guns were able to fire two to three rounds per minute.
68	In contrast, shells lobbed by very long-range artillery guns contained smaller quantities of explosives. For example, the shells hurled by the Krupp howitzer nicknamed 'Big Bertha', which bombarded Paris from the forest of Compiègne in the summer of 1918, contained only 6 per cent explosives. It is true that the desired impact was above all psychological in nature.
69	If we consider that France and its allies won the First World War, then we must recognize that the Socialist weapons minister Albert Thomas (1878–1932) played a role in this victory as significant as that of the eight generals raised to the supreme rank of Marshal of France after the war.
70	This explains why, given the proportion of ordnance remaining unexploded (between 10 and 15 per cent), active shells continue to be unearthed a century later. French demining teams still have decades of work ahead of them.
71	Gérard Guicheteau and Jean-Claude Simoën, *Les*

années sanglantes, 1914–1918 (Paris: Fayard, 2006), p. 64.
72 It seems that they also frequently carried this load in combat. Concerned that their soldiers not be separated from their kit by battle events, many officers ordered their men not to remove their packs at the start of an engagement.
73 Terence Zuber, *The Battle of the Frontiers: Ardennes, 1914* (Charleston, SC: History Press, 2007), pp. 30–1.
74 See Chapter 2.
75 Jean-Jacques Becker, 'Entrées en guerre', in Stéphane Audoin-Rouzeau and Jean-Jacques Becker, eds, *Encyclopédie de la Grande Guerre, 1914–1918: histoire et culture* (Paris: Bayard, 2004).
76 Holger H. Herwig, *The Marne, 1914: The Opening of World War I and the Battle That Changed the World* (New York: Random House, 2009), p. 61.
77 Gérard Guicheteau and Jean-Claude Simoën, *Les années sanglantes, 1914–1918* (Paris: Fayard, 2006), pp. 33–5.
78 Albert I was particularly exasperated by the fact that the German ultimatum, which was addressed to him personally, took the trouble to remind him of his family's German origins.
79 At the time, Belgium's active army consisted of 117,000 men. Mobilization would bring this figure to about 200,000, to which must be added the garrison personnel at the forts of Liège, Namur and Antwerp, as well as the militiamen of the Garde Civique.
80 John Horne and Alan Kramer, *German Atrocities, 1914: A History of Denial* (New Haven, CT: Yale University Press, 2001), p. 14.
81 See Chapter 8.
82 Anthony Clayton, *Paths of Glory: The French Army, 1914–18* (London: Cassell, 2005), pp. 6–7.
83 For the contemporary reader, there are a number of striking similarities between this testimony and

that given by top bank executives at the US Senate hearings during the 2008 financial crisis.
84   Quoted in André Bach, *Fusillés pour l'exemple: 1914–1915* (Paris: Tallandier, 2003), pp. 128–9.
85   Quoted ibid..
86   The regiment newsletters speak of covering 130 kilometres in twenty-hour periods. After a week of roaming in this manner, the cavalry corps would be virtually prevented from advancing any further by the urgent need to obtain more than 15,000 horseshoes.
87   It was also in Dinant that the German troops, once they had captured the city and seething with the excitement of these initial confrontations, proceeded to carry out the largest single massacre during the entire war of Belgian civilians (more than 600 gunned down, burned alive or drowned).
88   In particular, French learned from Lanrezac that the Germans had already crossed the Meuse. Shocked at hearing this, because Joffre had asserted the contrary, and stumbling through in his execrable schoolboy French, he had asked why, to which an exasperated Lanrezac responded, 'To go fishing, of course!'
89   It is important to note that, in the absence of conscription, the British Expeditionary Force comprised nearly all of the British territorial forces available in Europe, including troops intended to combat a possible invasion of Great Britain.
90   It should be recalled that, under the French military system, each army corps consisted of two infantry divisions, plus a varying number of cavalry and artillery units. And each army had between two and six corps. The French Second Army had four, corresponding to a total of about 180,000 men.
91   See Jean-Yves Le Naour, *Désunion nationale: la légende noire des soldats du Midi* (Paris: Vendémiaire, 2011), p. 18.

92 · See Stéphane Audoin-Rouzeau, *Les armes et la chair: trois objets de mort en 1914–1918* (Paris: Armand Colin, 2009), pp. 15–55.

93 XV Corps, at the time consisting in large part of recruits from the region of Nice (which had been part of France for less than fifty years), would be singled out for blame by the French general staff, and by Joffre in particular.

94 Robert A. Doughty, *Pyrrhic Victory: French Strategy and Operations in the Great War* (Cambridge, MA: Harvard University Press, 2008).

95 It was on 20 August outside Morhange that Castelnau, the Second Army's commander, lost one of his sons. His other two sons would also be killed in the war.

96 The French troops would leave the town in methodical fashion nevertheless, parading to the strains of La Marche Lorraine.

97 Brussels would be taken without resistance on 20 August.

98 In France at this time, an army usually consisted of four corps, but Joffre, in a sign of the weight he attached to this offensive, ordered one army corps each to be transferred from the Second and Fifth Armies.

99 At this point early in the war, army corps were constituted on the basis of uniformly local recruitment, along with the reservists assigned to these same depots. Each army corps was therefore marked by a very strong regional character. There were two main consequences of this initial homogeneity. First, the very heavy losses during the first weeks of the war would impact the young male population of a limited number of municipalities. Second, the reputations acquired – good or bad, whether justified or not – as a result of the conduct under fire of certain units would have an impact on the image of each region on the national level.

100 Jean Moreau, Éric Labayle and Jean-Louis Philippart,

Rossignol, *22 août 1914: journal du commandant Jean Moreau, chef d'état-major de la 3e division coloniale: suivi des témoignages du lieutenant Chaumel et du colonel Guichard-Montguers* (Parçay-sur-Vienne: Anovi, 2002), pp. 54–5.

101 An army corps would normally cover a front extending over eight to ten kilometres. The difficult relief of the Ardennes led the width of advancing columns of troops to be somewhat narrower. This is an important issue when we take into account the fact that an army corps numbers nearly 40,000 men (including about 30,000 combatants), who must move forward on routes where the infantry march in columns four men across.

102 Uncle of the future Marshal Leclerc and father of Pierre de Hauteclocque, a future Compagnon de la Libération. He would be killed later in the day, as would Bernard, another of his sons.

103 Among them that of Lieutenant Germain Foch of the 113th Infantry Regiment, son of the future marshal. His father would only learn of his death, together with that of his son-in-law, killed the same day in Lorraine, on 13 September, following the Battle of the Marne.

104 The barbed-wire fences were installed by local farmers, and not by the Germans.

105 See Bruce Gudmundsson, 'Unexpected Encounter at Bertrix', in Robert Cowley, ed., *The Great War: Perspectives on the First World War* (New York: Random House, 2003), pp. 21–xx.

106 Ministère de la guerre, État-major des Armées, Service historique, *Les armées françaises dans la Grande Guerre* (Paris: Imprimerie Nationale, 1922), pp. 428–9.

107 See André Bach, *Fusillés pour l'exemple: 1914–1915* (Paris: Tallandier, 2003).

108 In the German interpretation of the war, the most dramatic event took place on 22 October 1914, during

the First Battle of Ypres. That day, two divisions made up largely of German volunteers, many of whom were students who had cancelled their deferment, attacked the Belgian port. It was defended by British professional soldiers, whose typically accurate rifle fire mowed down a generation of German schoolboys and university students who had thrown themselves into the assault, singing 'Deutschland über Alles' in the fog. This episode has entered the German historical tradition under the term *Kindermord bei Ypern* ('slaughter of the innocents at Ypres').

109 And led them to commit numerous atrocities against Belgian civilians. See Chapter 8.
110 Although these two army corps would arrive in East Prussia too late to take part in the triumphant Battle of Tannenberg.
111 Quoted in Bach, *Fusillés pour l'exemple*, p. 137.
112 Ibid., p. 141.
113 Ibid., p. 141.
114 Total British losses at Waterloo amounted to 8,500 men out of an army of 32,000. At Le Cateau, the corresponding figures would be 7,800 men out of an army of 40,000.
115 See Appendix 3 for a reproduction of the dispatch of 6 September 1914, which gives an idea of the tone employed by Joffre: each unit is required to 'hold its ground, regardless of cost, even if this means getting its men killed on the spot'.
116 But Lanrezac would be fired as commander of the Fifth Army on 3 September and replaced by Franchet d'Espèrey.
117 Including the celebrated episode of the 'taxis of the Marne'.
118 Once the front had been stabilized and up until the final German offensive in May 1918, at no point, despite the blood spilled, did the front move more than twenty kilometres compared to its position in October 1914.

119 John Horne and Alan Kramer, *German Atrocities, 1914: A History of Denial* (New Haven, CT: Yale University Press, 2001), p. 74.
120 See Stéphane Audoin-Rouzeau, *L'enfant de l'ennemi, 1914–1918: viol, avortement, infanticide pendant la Grande Guerre* (Paris: Aubier, 1995).
121 Horne and Kramer, *German Atrocities, 1914*, p. 141.
122 Quoted ibid., p. 142 (slightly reworked for clarity).
123 Quoted ibid., p. 151.
124 See Isabel V. Hull, *Absolute Destruction: Military Culture and the Practices of War in Imperial Germany* (Ithaca, NY: Cornell University Press, 2005).
125 The name given by Westerners to the Chinese secret society called Yihetuan ('Righteous and Harmonious Fists'), which trained its members in the martial arts, and especially Chinese ritual boxing, thought to make them invulnerable to bullets.
126 Wilhelm II, 'Hun Speech' [1900], trans. Thomas Dunlap, GHDI [website]. Speech given by Kaiser Wilhelm II at Bremerhaven on 27 July 1990. Available at http://germanhistorydocs.ghi-dc.org/sub_document.cfm?document_id=755&language=english.
127 Quoted in Gewald Jan-Bart, *Herero Heroes: A Sociopolitical History of the Herero of Namibia, 1890–1923* (Athens, OH: Ohio University Press, 1998), p. 172.
128 Helmut Bley, *South-West Africa under German Rule, 1894–1914* (Evanston, IL: Northwestern University Press, 1971), p. 167.
129 Spencer C. Tucker, ed., *The Encyclopedia of the Spanish–American and Philippine–American Wars: A Political, Social, and Military History* (Santa Barbara, CA: ABC-CLIO, 2009), p. 693.
130 See Hull, *Absolute Destruction*, pp. 153–4. Hull compares the individual daily rations doled out to enemy civilians by British and German military in West Africa.
131 As would later be the case for IG Farben at Auschwitz.

132 Whose work would be cited in 1923 by Hitler in *Mein Kampf* and who counted among his students none other than Josef Mengele, the chief physician in charge of similar experiments at Auschwitz.
133 *Stenographische Berichte über die Verhandlungen des Deutschen Reichstages* [Stenographic minutes of German Reichstag debates], vol. 202, p. 4104 (30 January 1905).
134 Georges Lefebvre, *La Grande Peur de 1789* (Paris: Armand Colin, 1932).
135 Ibid..
136 Horne and Kramer, *German Atrocities*, 1914, pp. 17–18.
137 For a detailed account of the events of 21 to 23 August in Tamines, see http://fr.wikipedia.org/wiki/Massacre_de_Tamines (in French).
138 George L. Mosse, *Fallen Soldiers: Reshaping the Memory of the World Wars* (New York: Oxford University Press, 1990), p. 11.
139 Ibid.
140 Until the end of 1914, a certain number of French soldiers, initially reacting in desperation to the German advance, would end up returning to their units, assisted by Belgian and French civilians. Another point in relation to these statistics is that the identification of those killed would take years. In truth, it is still ongoing.
141 Sophie Delaporte, *Les médecins dans la Grande Guerre* (Paris: Bayard, 2003).
142 It is always exhausting, and technically difficult, to come to the aid of a soldier wounded in combat. In recognition of the difficulty of this task, the Israeli army, for example, makes its selection among applicants for officer school in part by observing their performance during first-aid drills.
143 Many accounts, as well as regimental logs, mention the surprise of combatants, thinking that they were on

the edge of the battlefield, outside the range of fire, on seeing the soldiers they were chatting with abruptly collapse, victims of a long-distance shot fired by an invisible enemy.

144   Although the British Royal Artillery lieutenant Henry Shrapnel invented the shell that bears his name in 1784, which would first be used on a massive scale in 1812 during Wellington's siege of Badajoz, the term would only enter common parlance as a result of its widespread use in the First World War.

145   Terence Zuber, *The Battle of the Frontiers: Ardennes, 1914* (Charleston, SC: History Press, 2007).

146   In any event, a certain number of accounts seem to indicate that German soldiers tended instead to use as their sighting point the sun's reflection on the mess tin attached to the top of the French infantryman's knapsack.

147   He thus became the eighty-eighth French soldier killed in action in this country since 2001. It is worth noting that France lost an average of more than 850 soldiers per day between 1914 and 1918.

148   Specifically the offensives in Artois (in the spring) and Champagne (in the autumn).

149   See Nicolas Le Nen, *Task Force Tiger: journal de marche d'un chef de corps français en Afghanistan* (Paris: Economica, 2010).

150   Following tradition as well as his own principles, Moltke waited to receive information from his subordinates. In September, exasperated at not having received any messages at all from his army commanders over the first four days of the Battle of the Marne, he dispatched a relatively young officer on his general staff, Lieutenant Colonel Richard Hentsch, to assess the situation. It was Hentsch who, on the basis of his observations and discussions with the army commanders, took it upon himself to order a general retreat.

151   Ministère de la guerre, État-major des Armées, Service historique, *Les armées françaises dans la*

Grande Guerre (Paris: Imprimerie Nationale, 1922), p. 399.

152 Raymond Poincaré, *Mémoires*, vol. 6, p. 276, quoted in Gérard Guicheteau and Jean-Claude Simoën, Les années sanglantes, 1914–1918 (Paris: Fayard, 2006), p. 145.

153 Foch, Pétain, Franchet d'Espèrey, Gallieni, Maunoury and Émile Fayolle would also be made Marshals of France.

Lightning Source UK Ltd.
Milton Keynes UK
UKHW021510191021
392423UK00001B/1